ANTIQUES
for
Amateurs
on a
Shoestring
Budget

ANTIQUES for Amateurs on a Shoestring Budget

by Marguerite Ashworth Brunner

BOBBS-MERRILL Indianapolis/New York

Published by The Bobbs-Merrill Company, Inc.
Indianapolis New York

Designed by Jill Weber
Manufactured in the United States of America

First printing

Library of Congress Cataloging in Publication Data

Brunner, Marguerite.
Antiques for amateurs on a shoestring budget.

Includes index.
1. Antiques. I. Title.
NK1125.B77 745.1 75-33534
ISBN 0-672-52059-1

To Sally and Sandy, my twin daughters,
without whose help this book could not have been written

CONTENTS

ONE

How to Start Collecting

1.

WHAT IS ANTIQUE?

In my nearly thirty years as an antique dealer, the question most frequently asked of me by young people has been "What is antique?" Almost daily I've had to explain to university students and other young people, embarking on their first antique collecting, the difference between just plain j-u-n-k and the j-u-n-q-u-e, as advertised by shops.

"How old is antique?" I've been asked. "Are those collectible Shirley Temple mugs and dolls really considered antique? How about the Buck Rogers Science Fiction comic books? Are the patchwork quilts, the churns and crocks used by our grandmothers really antiques, too?" Since there is no cut and dried answer to their questions, I've usually pointed out that there are few American dealers who wouldn't go out of their way to buy these things, and many shops would have to close their doors and go out of business if they stopped selling these "soon-to-be" antiques.

The United States Customs defines antique as anything made at least one hundred years before entry into the United States, and removes all import duties from them. The dictionary simply defines the word as something old compared to something new.

The very question, "What is an antique?" has always haunted the experts. Some connoisseurs, like Russell Carrell, who supervises fine antique shows in New York, hate seeing objects from the twenties and thirties flooding the markets and being snapped up by dealers and collectors alike. His theory is that authentic handmade antiques must pre-date 1850—or the end of the industrial revolution. He insists that a hundred years is too short a time for measuring antiques, and it encompasses too many manufactured pieces. He deplores the fact that a lot of junk, or mere secondhand stuff, is commanding ridiculously high prices today under the guise of antiques.

I disagree with Mr. Carrell. Much of the furniture from the early 1900's is more interesting and adaptable to modern apartments and houses than earlier pieces, say from the Empire era around 1830. Much of our most ornate and beautiful glass and silver has been produced within the last hundred years, and the craftsmanship that went into a piece of furniture, glass or silver enhances its value more than the age. Besides, if we removed objects less than a hundred years old from antique shops, most of them would have to go out of business for need of stock.

Victorian pieces, embracing the years of Queen Victoria's reign, 1837 to 1901, are perhaps the most popular pieces of furniture and bric-a-brac being sold in America today, and though items dating from the "late" Victorian period, the 1890's to 1901, are less than a hundred years old, they are definitely considered to be antiques.

The popular oaks and walnuts (round single pedestal tables, curved-front china cabinets, sideboards and washstands) from the early 1900's—especially from around 1920 through the 1930's—are becoming more valuable and harder to find each year. These pieces too are considered antiques by many, so the technical definition is not essentially the yardstick accepted by American dealers and collectors, except for purposes of importing things duty free.

N. H. Mager, collector, producer of antique shows and flea markets for almost three decades, agrees with me. He finds the hundred-year-old distinction a bit artificial and thinks an antique should

Round oak table, cut down, circa 1920. Bought with damaged veneer for $5. (Photo by Ross Chapple)

merely be something made before the present time. He displays much art that came into being in the twenties and thirties, and finds a big demand for Depression glass, old milk cans, cheaper dolls than the old German and French bisques, colored glass and bottles.

"A collector of these antiques-in-the-making," says Mr. Mager, "is actually no different from a collector of Meissen porcelain or Chippendale furniture. He sets out to learn as much as possible about his chosen field, then buys everything he can find in his favorite pattern. Before long he is not only helping generate a new

Washstand, poplar and maple, circa 1920. Bought painted for $15 in 1974. (Photo by Ross Chapple)

collecting fashion, he is creating scarcity, running prices up and becoming an investor as well as a collector by increasing the value of his collection."

There are more shops in America today selling these new collectibles than are selling authentic antiques. The prices are within the budgets of young collectors, and these pieces will certainly increase in value as time passes.

While some shops and galleries still won't touch these things, Sotheby Parke Bernet, America's finest auction gallery, has opened its doors to American antiques and 19th and 20th century objects.

Mr. Timothy Tetlow, speaking for the gallery, says that they used to skim off the valuable pieces from estates and send the rest to lesser galleries. But in the past few years, they have seen a great demand for Americana, extending as late as our own century. Mr. Timothy Tetlow thinks this is a good thing: "Just because an object is antique doesn't mean it is desirable. Quality is quality. It's time we made the distinction between what is good and what is shoddy, instead of how old or rare it is. Buyers should base their evaluation on the object's appeal, its artistic merit, its craftsmanship and its utility."

If you're an amateur and wondering whether a piece you're interested in is really an antique, you might consider this rule that comes from another prominent antique dealer: "If you like it and it has reached 'voting age,' buy it. I've bought and sold thousands of items operating on this principle, and I've made a very good living for fifty years."

More and more experts are beginning to agree that an antique is merely something beautiful from the past—something that has mellowed with age and is pleasing to the beholder. Thus more and more items from the 19th and 20th centuries are being sought by amateur and professional collectors alike, for they are plentiful and not too expensive and have ways of turning up in strange and unusual places, all the way from garbage dumps to the most respectable antique shops.

The main thing to realize is that almost anything you like can be collectible—and collectibles need not be old, rare or expensive to become valuable. In fact, your collection may well turn out to be more profitable than any investment you can make. Just for example, my family and I lived comfortably for a full year on the proceeds from a collection of thirty-five oil paintings. A close friend of mine sent three sons through college on twelve house-sales a year. She collected anything and everything old, often trading a very good piece for many "slightly antique" pieces, and once a month she had a sale in her home. She planned it for the weekend right after the first of the month, for she lived in a "government" town, where most folks were paid on the first, and that's when they had money for buying her things.

Another woman I know collected china all her working years, and on retirement sold her entire collection to finance a trip around the world. Anybody with a little time can start a collection of old things and one day surprise the family with extra money for something special they've always wanted to do.

With most of us, collecting begins in childhood. Small boys and girls start out collecting marbles or baseball cards from bubble gum packages, dolls or miniature cups and saucers and a score of other appealing things. Or perhaps they become avid collectors of coins or stamps.

It is a wise parent who switches a child's interest from collecting junk to collecting things of value. From cheap dimestore dolls, children may be steered into collecting dolls of the world and later to antique dolls, learning along the way some of the history surrounding them—an educational process made interesting.

Most of my customers have been amateurs under thirty years old, most of them on shoestring budgets. In this book I hope to pass along some of the tips and short-cuts to collecting that I've learned and have been passing on to them over the years.

2.

LEARNING ABOUT ANTIQUES—THE HARD WAY

There is no easy way to learn about antiques. It is, I've discovered, an art of trial and error, an absorbing game and a profitable hobby that often pays better dividends than stocks and bonds. If you're the worrying type who loses sleep over mistakes, it can also be nerve-racking. The most successful collectors are those who acquire a sort of gambling spirit—you will lose some and win some, but tomorrow is always another day, another adventure, and you can profit from all your mistakes.

I sort of stumbled into the antique business. At the time I knew absolutely nothing about furniture. I had furnished my apartment in Fairlington, Virginia, with second-hand pieces simply because I couldn't afford new ones. I bought pieces because I liked them or because they fitted into a special place in my rooms. I was a newspaper woman at the time, happy with my job, and didn't dream that before the year was out I'd be in business for myself—a business about which I knew less than the rankest amateur.

It started because a friend in the Navy was a photographer and wanted very much to go into business for himself, so I invested $5,000 in photographic equipment for him and took a longterm lease on a commercial property in Arlington, Virginia. We soon discovered that wartime restrictions made it impossible to get film wholesale or to process a roll of film for a customer without allowing him to buy another roll for future use. Ours would have been primarily a processing business, and naturally we received no business at all. We tried commercial photography, but failed before we even got off the ground.

There I was, stuck with a large building in the high-rent district, and an expensive apartment whose lease had just about expired. To try to salvage my investment, I gave up the apartment and moved into the business property. Setting up a small apartment on the top floor, I decided to sub-lease the bottom floor as offices. I had too much furniture for my two rooms, so I ran an advertisement in the classified section of the *Washington Star* to sell the remaining pieces. The response was terrific. Within a few hours after the paper hit the streets, I'd not only sold every piece of my furniture, but had people begging for duplicates. One man went after the woman who'd bought my old library table, offering her three times what she'd paid for it.

I took names and phone numbers that day, listing the things people wanted and what they were willing to pay. I really thought I could do it part-time, acting as a shopper on my days off from the newspaper. When I went to the Arlington County Courthouse to secure a license to sell retail, I found that I had to estimate my sales for the remaining seven months of the year. The license fee was figured on that estimate in the beginning, and based on your actual sales the following years. I set what I thought was a very high figure, $10,000, but by December I had actually sold forty-seven thousand dollars' worth of furniture and had become a full-time dealer.

Those were exciting months, and filled with mistakes. I still had no idea of dealing in antiques. I think the Chippendale chair disaster is what changed my mind and set me on the path to learning all I could about old things. At public auction I bought six old mahogany dining chairs for $2 each. They were not especially pretty, for the finish was so old and dark you couldn't see the grain of the wood.

They were dainty in design, however, and I decided to take the finish off and put them together with a dining table to be sold as a unit. It was still wartime, and good furniture was hard to come by. Dealers in new furniture told me the Navy had bought up all the good furniture glue for ship building, and new furniture coming out of the factories wasn't worth carting home—after a few months in heated houses and apartments, the drawers would shrink, and glued sides often separated altogether.

My mahogany chairs were very sturdy and I knew I could sell them quickly, if I refinished them. I moved them to the front porch of my shop and spread out newspapers before beginning my first refinishing job. Just as I started to brush paint remover on the first chair, a well-dressed woman came and parked in the driveway. She literally threw up her hands in horror when she saw what I was about to do. "Don't touch them," she screamed at me, "they're perfect, just as they are!"

I looked at her in astonishment—how could such old, beatup chairs be perfect? She asked what I'd take for them, examining them one by one. Since she seemed so excited, I decided to ask an outrageous price: "I'll take a hundred dollars for the set as is."

Without hesitation, she said, "I'll take them," and promptly wrote a check. I gladly loaned her blankets to cover them so she could carry them in her car, for I was so happy at my profit on this sale. Imagine—I'd made more on those six chairs than in a whole week working on the *Times-Herald!*

Although she promised to return my blankets, I really didn't expect to see her again. I might never have become an antique dealer if she hadn't come back a week later and announced casually that she'd sold my Chippendale chairs for $1,000, crated. That was when I learned that a ball and claw foot on a chair was a Chippendale design, and that original antiques are not necessarily pretty.

From that day on, I borrowed or bought every book I could find on antique furniture. I learned about Hepplewhite and Sheraton and Duncan Phyfe, about the periods of furniture and how to spot a hand-crafted piece. I learned that the Empire was called the "bastard" period, and that these pieces were undesirable because of their bulk, despite their handmade dovetails and beautiful veneers. I also learned that by knocking off the posts in front of many Empire cupboards and chests, and stripping off the veneers with a wet cloth and hot iron I could produce beautiful Early American pieces of walnut, cherry and pine. Many American Empire pieces were made of as many as three different woods, and because they were undesirable in their original state could be purchased for as little as $5.

I got my first Empire chest for $2, because the veneer was half gone from the drawers. This made it easier for me, since I planned to take it all off anyway. I sold that piece for $200 in my first antique show.

Another one of my big mistakes occurred that same year. I never thought to look over old pieces for hidden compartments or places where money or valuables might have been stashed for safekeeping. I know now that in the old days many people were afraid of banks and used all sorts of hiding places. Later, when the banks failed during the Depression, people again distrusted banks, and hid their money as their parents had done before them. In this case I bought a brass poster bed from an old lady who was breaking up house after her husband's death and going to California to live. Although I polished it up, it never occurred to me to remove the balls on top of the bedposts and examine the hollow insides. I sold that bed for $40, and later learned that a roll of old currency (the big bills) had been found inside one of the posts. My customer would not tell me how much money it was, but the big currency was collectible even then, back in the forties.

Later on, in a secret drawer of a desk I bought at an auction outside of Pittsburgh, I found a rosary case containing two diamond rings. I received more for the two rings than I did for the desk. Around that time a dealer I knew found a can of old coins inside a Ben Franklin stove he had bought from a charity thrift shop—so, you see, it does pay to look for hidden treasures in old things. A favorite old hiding place was behind pictures. Dealers are all aware of this, and you will seldom find an old picture whose backing has not been torn off.

If you're interested in furniture, it's a good idea to start learning as much as you can about the various kinds of wood. There are many similarities between them, and amateurs may find this confusing. Oak and chestnut look very much alike, as do cherry and mahogany, pine and poplar. There are differences, however, and these are important in determining just how good an old piece of furniture is. The likenesses between some woods fool even dealers, so amateurs shouldn't be discouraged if they find it difficult at first to tell the difference between them.

For instance, a friend of mine who had been an antique dealer for many years bought a huge cabinet with double glass doors to use as a display cabinet in her shop. The cabinet was tall, reaching the ceiling, and she bought it for $35 (including delivery) from one of the thrift stores.

One day when I happened to be there, an elderly, well-dressed man came in. He was enchanted with that cabinet, and although she told him repeatedly it was not for sale, he insisted he had to have it and started to write a check. My friend was becoming annoyed when he said, "Surely you can't turn down twenty-five hundred dollars for it?"

The moral of this story is that we both believed the cabinet was oak. It had been purchased as oak and the grain looked like oak—but it was really chestnut, which is more valuable. The man who bought it turned out to be a decorator who was doing over a big house, and this particular piece was something he had scoured the country to find.

Woods are a fascinating study in themselves, and they tell you a great deal about furniture. If it is an American piece, it is most likely made of American wood—the real antiques, that is. Most early American furniture was made of pine, walnut, cherry or poplar. The earliest pieces were often made of wood grown right on the builder's land, the trees being cut down, the boards planed and sanded to specifications. That is why most primitive pieces had solid sides and were built with thicker boards than later machine-made ones. Only the very wealthy could afford imported woods in the early days.

There were several centers—notably Philadelphia, Charleston, South Carolina, and Baltimore—where cabinet makers constructed the finest furniture, often copying English designs. It was not unusual for a man to become a carver, working on furniture made by other craftsmen. Most of these carved pieces were made of mahogany and walnut.

Once you know a little something about wood you can start looking for good pieces under coats of paint. This is where you're more likely to find something valuable for very little, since many dealers find refinishing too expensive to be worth it to them. Look inside the drawers and on unpainted surfaces (underneath or in back) and see if you can determine the wood beneath the paint.

Woods give us a pretty good idea if a piece is really old, for they mellow with age; if you've ever refinished a piece of furniture, you can readily tell the difference between "green" wood and seasoned wood that has weathered many years. I love old woods. They are beautiful even without finishes. When we've restored old pieces we've often given them a clear satin finish or simply waxed them repeatedly with beeswax. One of my customers put it aptly when she said, "It's so easy to fall in love with a pretty piece of wood—each one seems to have a character all its own."

The easiest way to learn to identify woods is to visit a cabinet maker and ask for small samples of wood of various kinds and compare them. If you don't know a cabinet maker, visit a lumber yard where the samples, although of new wood, will help you to learn to distinguish the different grains.

For beginning furniture collectors, the public library is a goldmine. There are two books, however, that I think are worth buying and keeping with you at all times. One is Thomas Ormsbee's paperback *Field Guide to Early American Furniture,* published by Little, Brown, Boston, and the other is Warman's *Price Guide,* which may be ordered from E. G. Warman, Uniontown, Pennsylvania. Keep these with you for ready reference on buying trips, but out of sight of the dealer. If the more experienced dealer sees you consulting them, he spots you immediately as an amateur, while the less experienced dealer (especially in thrift shops) may think that the book has told you that an item is valuable, and either raise the price or refuse to sell it to you at all.

Visit museums and historical homes open to the public. Many authentic antiques, aged well beyond the hundred years, may be seen in these. Make sketches, take notes and never fail to ask questions, when possible. Compare what you see with pictures in the books you study. Once I owned a corner cupboard that was identical to one I saw in Robert E. Lee's mansion in Arlington. I was able to raise my price substantially when I could tell a customer to look at them both and compare, for there was a very good chance they might have been made by the same cabinet maker.

The exciting part of antiquing is that you participate in your hobby while you're learning. You'll make mistakes, as I did—but your mistakes should not be costly, for it is never wise for an amateur to start out with expensive pieces. A good rule is to become a browser in expensive shops and a buyer in thrift shops.

Another good rule is to keep a diary of your antiques. It is of the utmost importance to keep complete records of every antique you buy, find or trade for—not only what the item cost, but the date of purchase and the circumstances, especially where it was obtained. Ask for and keep receipts whenever possible. Thrift shops and rummage sales do not give receipts, so it is important to write down all the pertinent information about each item. This way you are protected if you should, inadvertently, buy stolen goods. It is easy to forget what you paid for something three or four years ago. The time may come when you want to sell it, and a record will be invaluable to you. Then, too, you may want to add your collection to your homeowners insurance policy, and for this it is wise to establish what your treasures are worth. If you make improvements on your antiques, make a note of money and time spent on them, for this must also be taken into account, if you decided to sell them. And some day, with luck and a little knowledge, you may find what we all dream of—a grimy, paint-covered table for $25 at some country auction, and after stripping the paint away, discover you have a 250-year-old find worth $1,000 or more. You just never know in this business when something like that may happen, and the important thing is to prepare yourself to recognize it when you see it.

3.

WHERE TO FIND ANTIQUES

What I call a shoestring budget is one that can afford perhaps ten or twenty dollars a month to be invested in collecting. Some of the most avid collectors are young people in their first jobs, with take-home pay of perhaps a hundred dollars a week or less, or students getting by on allowances from home or perhaps on part-time employment—and, naturally, they don't go antiquing in exclusive shops and galleries. It doesn't take a lot of money to begin or add to antique collections if you know where to look, and it's twice as much fun finding a treasure for practically nothing.

Here is a list of the most likely sources for antiques that cost very little. I have deliberately left auctions until last, for they have many pitfalls for the amateur which need to be explained.

THRIFT SHOPS

Thrift shops are the best sources for bargains, and shops sponsored by churches and charitable organizations are first on my list. The smaller the shop, the better. The main stores of the Salvation

Army, Saint Vincent de Paul, Goodwill and other organizations have experts pricing their older items, and you may well pay more there than in regular antique shops. Visit their smaller outlets, where many donations are brought directly to the stores and priced by volunteer help who change from day to day and do not always recognize an antique as such. Most of these smaller shops depend on clothing sales for their money, and when they do have older, more valuable pieces of china, glass, silver and furniture, they price them low.

Privately owned thrift shops are also excellent sources, for most of them are operating on a shoestring and must sell daily to stay in business. I used to find that these shops have their best buys around the first of the month, when the rent was due. Very few of these dealers really know antiques (as I didn't in the beginning) and will most likely travel the same path I did in learning—so the newer the shop and the less experienced the dealer, the more likely you are to make a find.

It is important to stress at this point that you should buy any antique that is cheap, whether or not you intend to collect that particular thing. The antique business is the greatest horse-trading business in the world, and any bargain you find may well be traded to another dealer for something you really want. It is almost impossible to build a valuable collection of anything without trading off items you don't want or need. It's wise, too, to find out what the dealers are looking for when you visit the better shops, for you may come across exactly the thing in some out-of-the-way thrift shop.

Learn the specific days when thrift shops receive their wares. Some of them rent trucks once or twice a week to pick up stock. By learning this about a mission store in North Carolina, I was able to buy beautiful rockers for as little as $3, collections of good books for less than 10 cents each, and many other valuable items. I made a point of being there when the truck was unloaded and buying before the items had been priced. Other dealers used to tell me the mission never had anything that was any good—of course they wouldn't find antiques there after a few dealers, like myself, had bought them off the truck.

Make friends with clerks in the thrift shops. I save all my used grocery bags and donate them to a shop in my area; shops like these cannot afford to buy new bags, so they will appreciate your discards. Let the clerks know what you are collecting, and after they become accustomed to your visits (it's wise to go on the same day each week, when possible, so they will be expecting you), they may put valuable pieces aside for you.

Always be honest with the dealers you visit. I tell them that I used to be a dealer, although I am not an expert. There is so much to know that there are few, if any, who are experts in all areas of antiques. Most dealers specialize in one particular category, such as Early American furniture, silver, oriental items, china, glass or dolls. When thrift shop clerks learn that you know something about old things, they may save an interesting item for you to see and tell them about. They've often let me set my own price on unusual pieces, because they trusted me and because I always offered more than I would have anywhere else.

GARAGE, BASEMENT AND YARD SALES

Most basement, garage and yard sales are held on weekends, so buy the Friday newspaper early. If your city has a bulldog edition that comes out at midnight the night before, by all means wait up for it. If a classified advertisement interests you and the hours are listed as ten to five, call them early and ask if you may come to the sale before hours. I've had potential customers call and give me all sorts of reasons why they couldn't come at the advertised hours—either they were going out of town, or wouldn't have a baby sitter, or they had out-of-town company, or they were just dying to come to the sale, but their planes were leaving early. . . .

If you want to get in before the sale starts and the merchandise is picked over, either ask permission to come early, or simply arrive and take along some household items you no longer want and offer them free to the person having the sale. Here, again, the seller will appreciate your grocery bags. If a neighbor is having a sale, offer to help her, either at the sale or by watching her children during it. There are many workable approaches.

RUMMAGE SALES

Almost every church has at least one big rummage sale a year. Look in the Yellow Pages of your telephone book, call the local churches and ask to be put on their mailing lists for the rummage sales. One church in Washington has a sale every October that lasts for three days. I know folks who come to them from out of town because the sales are so tremendous. I've bought old tapestries for $2, sterling silver jewelry for a dime—and so many other collectibles that it would be impossible to mention them all. For this particular sale I always arrive an hour before the doors open and wait, first in line, to get in. It is wise to take shopping bags with you, and very helpful to take along a friend who can help you carry them around. I always buy a lot of books, and they are heavy. Then, too, a friend can take your purchases to your car as you make them, so you aren't burdened down with so many packages.

Remember, too, that items come in continually at rummage sales. Members of the church often bring in things all during the sale, and if it lasts more than one day, a storage room may hold lots of new merchandise to be put out as the sale progresses. My best buys have come from rummage sales, for the time is so limited and everything must be sold; therefore the prices are low.

NEWSPAPER WANT ADS

Many beginners look only under "Antiques for Sale" in the classified section of their newspapers. This is a mistake. Pay special attention to advertisements that read: "Household furnishings for sale. Moving. Everything must be sold." I've found a lot of good buys in these. Almost every household has a few antiques, something that belonged to a relative or was given them when they first started housekeeping. If people have modern furniture and dislike old things, they usually value them very low; and then, too, you may find a valuable piece that the seller doesn't even know is old or worth anything. Once I attended a house sale where I found a bisque piano doll in a little girl's play box. Her parents considered it just another ordinary doll.

A friend and I went to an apartment sale recently and discovered a lovely old rosewood piano that the owner planned to leave there because it was too expensive to move and he couldn't believe anybody would want to buy such a heavy piece. He gave it to us for the taking. My friend knew a woman looking for an inexpensive piano to take lessons on, and we sold her that piano for $150.

I have known housewives with more time than money who would go into a house or apartment after people had moved out and clean up the place for any unwanted pieces of furniture and bric-a-brac that had been left behind. A small inexpensive advertisement in the personal column of your local newspaper to "put a house in order in exchange for unwanted items" may open many profitable doors for you. Then, too, if there are pieces you don't want, you may get permission to have a sale right in that house or apartment, adding some of your own things to build it up.

Frequently, people who don't want to be bothered with selling their household goods will be happy to have someone else conduct the sale, splitting the take down the middle.

ANTIQUE SPECIALTY SHOPS

If a shop specializes in silver or glass, ask to see picture frames or some piece of furniture not on display. Almost all shops have a back room or storage area where dealers put things they do not care too much about. Ask for something you don't see and you may be invited into the back room, where you may find a real bargain. Antique dealers cannot always buy only the specific item they want, for many things are sold in job lots. Also, a dealer may buy a whole houseful of antiques in order to get a few good things and will usually sell unwanted items for very little. For instance, a dealer I knew in Pittsburgh had a working arrangement with a bank to buy entire estates. Her specialty was furniture, and I bought a beautiful set of Haviland china from one of her estates for $20, because she rarely sold china or glass. So, in specialty shops, always ask for the opposites. You may be pleasantly surprised at what the dealer will turn up.

CONSIGNMENT SHOPS

In many consignment shops, the owner is allowed to set his own prices. Since these dealers handle such a variety of stock, including clothing, they can't be expected to know the value of everything they sell. This leaves room for bargaining. If you see a consignment piece you really want and think the price is too high, have the dealer call the owner and make an offer. Frequently the owner will come down, especially if the piece has been in the shop for a while.

The consignment shop is a good outlet for you, too, when you have items you no longer want or need. The money you make this way will help you finance the antiques you are looking for. Most shops send out their checks once a month, and if you have items in several of these shops, you can count on a steady monthly income. The shop usually takes 20% to 30% of the sale price, which is a good deal for you, for you have no overhead in selling your things.

VOLUNTEER WORK

I'll never understand how my name is always picked for jury duty and volunteer work, but it is. Every time there is a cancer or heart fund or any other drive, I am always called and I've never learned to say no. At first, I helped out because I felt I had so much to be thankful for—but when I found a beautiful old pine hutch on somebody's side porch (and bought it for $10), I started ringing doorbells with anticipation. Every house had a potential treasure just waiting for me. I've bought china, cut glass, an oil painting and numerous other treasures on these fund-raising drives. I've learned that almost everybody has something to sell, and what better way is there to get into homes than by doing volunteer work for a worthy cause?

CLEAN-UP DRIVES

Every city and town has a clean-up drive once or twice a year. That's when people set out on the curb all the old things they want to get rid of, and the city picks them up on a certain day. I've found sterling silver flatware, old linens, a three-piece Victorian parlor set (needing upholstering), an old Victrola and numerous other things in such clean-up drives. Don't worry about rummaging through the trash, for I've seen well-dressed folks with their station wagons and trucks making the rounds before pickup day. You wouldn't believe the beautiful things people throw away. Some folks wrap their things in tissue paper, as though making a gift of them. I got $100 once, in Pittsburgh, for a beautiful, discarded Oriental rug my husband dragged five blocks to our shop. Today, that rug would be worth a small fortune. Cities often sell those good things themselves, and so many dealers were making the rounds in Pittsburgh that year, rummaging through beforehand, that the police were told to stop them.

If you live in a city, you may also find trunks, chests and many other valuable items sitting on the curb or in alleys for the trash man to pick up. Just recently I saw a boxful of old 78-rpm records sitting beside the trash bags near my home. I took it home and found among them several John McCormack and Schumann-Heink records that are definitely collector's items.

DRIVES OFF THE BEATEN PATH

A drive through the country may turn up more treasure than you'd dream. Many people who live in the backwoods have furniture piled up in their yards or stacked against a barn. Once I found a brass bed, tarnished black, leaning against a fence as I drove along a country road. I bought it for $5, and I'm sure the farmer who sold it to me was delighted with his price for what he considered a pile of junk. Another time, my daughters and I drove down a country road trying to find homes for three kittens. We stopped at a shack where an elderly couple were sitting on the front porch. They had no electricity, and when the old man heard my daughter's transistor radio, he was fascinated. The couple not only took two of the kittens, they traded me a beautiful, handmade pie safe for the transistor, which I replaced for less than $5. The pie safe was pegged, in perfect condition, and I sold it in my shop a few days later for $150. This is a good way to buy old iron washpots, kettles and such things, for they are often kept outside country houses and can be seen from the road.

AUCTIONS

A fast-moving auction sale is, in many respects, like a bargain basement sale at Macy's. If you're an amateur, beware! I once scratched my nose at a Post Office auction in Washington, D.C., and ended up buying a mailhamperful of stationery. Dealers have ways of nodding their heads, blinking their eyes or putting a finger beside their noses to raise their bids, and if the amateur isn't careful during

The way auctions were conducted in the late 1800's. This one by Sloan's predecessor at 11th and Pennsylvania Avenue N.W., Washington, D.C. (Photo courtesy C. G. Sloan's Auction House)

spirited bidding, he may well end up with something he neither wants nor can afford. Nothing angers an auctioneer more than having someone renege on a bid, and in many auction houses, if this happens, you are forbidden to bid again.

Webster defines an auction as a sale in which the owner of property obliges himself, under certain conditions, to transfer his property to the highest bidder. What Mr. Webster doesn't tell you is that an auction can induce a fever—a sort of mass hysteria and excitement that can fire the imagination and loosen the purse strings. It's easy for dealers, as well as amateurs, to become reckless at an auction. Here, all sales are final! You buy "as is." If you discover later that you've bought damaged goods, you're out of luck.

Along with the excitement of an auction sale there is a sadness, too—seeing portraits of another era being sold for their frames, seeing photograph albums and fine family Bibles passing into strange hands.

My worst experiences at auctions have been with theft—once property is sold, the house is not responsible. I learned to remove the cabinet keys from chests and dining pieces, any unattached parts, and quickly claim all books, bric-a-brac and jewelry the minute I purchased them. Once I had all the tubes stolen from a television set that was actually working at the time of the sale. A friend of mine always removed the doors from small commodes and cushions from chairs and sofas. You've lost a great deal of money if you discover the sofa you bought for $100 is minus a cushion on delivery. For this reason, most dealers who buy regularly from an auction house will pay one of the house employees to remove their purchases to a safe place immediately. If you are an amateur, you should never go to an auction alone. Take along a friend to watch your purchases or hold the small items if you intend to buy more.

There is so much thievery at auctions that it is a fact that we must reckon with. Once I bought a huge lot of books from an estate for a great deal of money, because there were several Civil War books among them. While I went to get packing boxes for them, someone stole every one of the Civil War items, and I ended up with run-of-the-mill books that hardly brought back my investment.

If you're not familiar with an auction house, you may discover that when the auctioneer asks for a $2 bid on a set of chairs, he actually means $2 for each piece. This is true of dining sets, bedroom sets and the like. Many houses ask for bids on each piece, and a ten-piece dining set you thought you were buying for $50 may turn out to cost you $500. It pays to observe many auction procedures before you actually participate in buying.

Every time a large auction is held, some history is placed on the block. Americans will travel hundreds of miles and sit on uncomfortable seats for hours on end to buy something that once belonged to a famous person. I learned early in the business that a good story will sell an antique piece quicker than a pretty finish. The most exciting auction I ever attended was in Winston-Salem, North Carolina, in 1967. All the personal belongings and fabulous art treasures of Hedda Hopper and Claude Rains were put on the auction block, and people came hundreds of miles to look and buy. That first day, many women came to buy fantastic Hedda Hopper hats, only to discover that they had all been given to her friends. One woman told me she had driven seventy miles just to buy a hat to impress her bridge club. Even though they were disappointed, I didn't see a single woman leave.

In many ways this auction was comparable to those held at Parke-Bernet Galleries in New York, and it was quite extraordinary for a small southern town. It was definitely not for amateurs, but it did offer them a wonderful opportunity to study more advanced collections of exceptional value. It always pays to visit every auction possible, observing the antiques and what they bring, noting any historical interest they may have—this is a valuable education in itself.

One of the most interesting auction houses I've ever visited is C. G. Sloan and Company in Washington, D.C., who since 1891 have auctioned off possessions of presidents, of the late Jerome Napoleon Bonaparte, great grandnephew of the emperor, of the

A typical Sloan's auction sale in Washington, D.C. (Photo courtesy C. G. Sloan's Auction House)

Calvert family, direct descendents of Lord Baltimore, as well as signed paintings by famous artists and possessions of congressmen and senators and other distinguished persons. At Sloan's, these sales happen often, and these rare pieces that belonged to famous persons don't always bring fantastic prices.

In 1972 I attended a Sloan's sale and bought a sixty-inch round dining table of solid walnut that came from the Decatur House (home of Stephen Decatur, directly across from the White House) for only $70. The apron of the table had been damaged, but my husband is an expert in refinishing and restoring, so that presented no problem. Before the sale was over, someone offered me $200 for it as it stood, and I would not sell. I knew its value and had a place for it in the old townhouse we were restoring. If I ever decide to sell it, I know I can get closer to $1,000 for it, for it is banquet size and will take ten leaves. Many presidents and other notables probably ate from my table. The massively carved pedestal is unique and very much in demand on today's market.

After the assassination of Abraham Lincoln, some of his effects were sold at Sloan's. His dining table reappeared there in 1926 and went for a measly $25.

When Chester A. Arthur took possession of the Executive Mansion in 1881, he so disliked the china and certain furnishings used by President Hayes that he ordered them sold by a local auctioneer. Washingtonians created such a fuss over this that it was later announced that no White House property would ever again be sold at public auction. Some of the Hayes china was acquired by Admiral George Dewey's wife. It remained in the Dewey family until 1933, when all of their furnishings (thirty-five rooms of it) were hauled off to Sloan's to be sold to the highest bidder. The Hayes china brought $3 a plate. A nest of tables, presented by the Emperor of Japan to Admiral Dewey, was sold for only $16. The walnut armchair, used as a desk chair aboard Dewey's flagship *Olympia,* was sold to the late Evelyn Walsh McLean of Hope Diamond fame for only $11.

Bargains can also be found in paintings. For example, James McNeil Whistler did not always sign his work with his signature. Instead, he often painted in a little butterfly. One of his paintings sold at Sloan's for $140, far less than its worth.

Dining table from the Decatur House, bought in 1972 from Sloan's Auction House for $70. (Photo by Ross Chapple)

American antiques have traveled extensively over our country. Dealers from the north go south to buy, and vice versa. Often the real buys are coated with paint and not easily recognized. The more primitive pieces of Early Americana have come into their own and demand good prices nowadays. However, many are within the reach of everyone, since they have weathered the years under coats and coats of paint.

At most auction houses, the red flag is posted outside the door on Sale day, a custom that comes from the Arabs. In ancient days, when Arabian tribes raided each other, they carried their loot to a central place, piled it high and perched a red flag on top. The flag was an invitation to buy, and it signified that everything in the pile was for sale. Auctions today as conducted so that each successive bid is higher than the preceding one, but it was not always so. In ancient days there was another process, called "Dutch Auction," which worked in reverse. A high price was placed on an object to be sold, and gradually reduced until a bid was obtained.

Our present system of auctioneering is the fairest known way to dispose of goods. In many states, when people die intestate, their possessions are auctioned off so their estates can be converted into cash. Their relatives must bid on the family heirlooms just like everyone else. So there will always be antiques for sale, as long as people continue to die without leaving wills.

In America anybody can hold an auction, and can auction off almost anything. Elvis Presley auctioned off an old bathtub, painted sea-blue, which he had once used, along with the oven that had cooked his food and a baseball glove he'd caught flies with, for the fantastic sum of $11,000—more than was brought by Abe Lincoln's table, President Hayes' china, the Dewey tables and the Whistler painting put together. But then, that's what makes auctions so much fun. You never know what will turn up, or how much it may bring.

TWO

The Collectibles

4.

GLASS

There are more collectors of glass than of anything else in the antique field. You will find collectors of cut, pressed, pattern, art or colored glass in homes with modern furnishings. Antique glass is pretty and often ornate. I've had customers who wouldn't give me a dime for antique furniture, and yet would pay outrageous prices for fine cut crystal.

The origin of glass-making is lost in antiquity. The Roman writer Pliny wrote that a band of Phoenician merchants inadvertently discovered glass-making while returning from Egypt. They landed on the coast of Palestine, camped on the sandy beach of the River Belus and built their fires, placing blocks of niter under their cooking pots. Later they discovered that the niter had melted and mingled with the sand to form a liquid stream that hardened into what we know as glass. This story has become a legend, even though Pliny failed to explain how so mild a heat as an open fire would produce what today requires intense heat in furnaces.

The earliest tableware glass was pressed by dropping a lump of liquid glass into an iron mold of the design wanted and pressing the mass into shape with a plunger. Much of it was made in two- or three-part molds; frequently the bowl of a goblet was shaped in one press, while the stem was done in another.

Americans became very glass-conscious during the 1873 World's Columbian Exposition in Chicago, when glass makers put on extensive exhibitions of their art. For the first time people saw glass spun into fabric by melting a glass rod in the flame of a blowpipe and drawing the melted thread over a wheel revolving at high speed. This created quite a stir as crowds watched spun glass woven into cloth for a dress for the Queen Regent of Spain. Newspapers called the process a miracle. The warp was white silk, the woof was glass, and they were woven together on a hand-loom.

Prior to World War I, Germany and Austria were the glass-making capitals of the world, but the war interrupted the industry there and the glass centers shifted to the United States. In the early 1920's there were several hundred glass factories in the United States, most of them located in the eastern and midwestern states of Ohio, Pennsylvania, West Virginia, Indiana, New York, New Jersey and Illinois.

There are various kinds of collectible glass, of which the finest is the etched and engraved lead crystal that commands the highest prices. Despite its delicacy, many pieces have survived the centuries and can be seen in museums around the world.

Much more accessible to the average collector are the various kinds of cut and pressed glass, and the fanciful art glass of recent times.

Most amateur collectors, I've discovered, would rather collect cut glass than pressed or pattern glass. Cut glass is beautiful, but not as valuable as most of the pressed and pattern glass preferred by more experienced collectors. It is heavier and comes in two varieties: hand cut and machine cut. Naturally, the hand cut is more desirable and the machine cut more plentiful. When pieces are both cut and pressed, they are called pressed cut.

CUT GLASS

Much cut glass is being imported from Europe these days. Some of it is beautiful and very hard to tell from our own older glass. On a trip to Florence, South Carolina, several years ago, I found a shop which sold only new imported glass and china. I bought some pieces of cut glass for $18 each (bowls, compotes, decanters) which I sold immediately upon my return for $25 each, despite their Czechoslovakian stickers, which I had left on. Of course I did not make a lot of money on them, but I knew they would sell quickly and I never pass up any pieces of pretty, salable glass. Other dealers would tell me it's bad business not to double your money, but I did a large volume and could afford to make less on some things.

PRESSED GLASS

Recently, I bought fifty pieces of heavy pressed glass from a supermarket in my neighborhood—and I saw other dealers buying it by the cartful. There were bowls, compotes, pitchers for 99 cents and goblets, desserts, glasses for 39 cents. It was a special offer that should have lasted thirty days, but the stock was depleted long before that time. Now, less than a month later, I could sell any one of the big pieces for $6 to $8, and I'd certainly get at least $1 on the goblets and glasses. The glass is heavy and beautiful and in a year or two will be worth a great deal more.

As I took it home I was reminded of the time in North Carolina when I bought all the candy dishes a supermarket got in just to make sure none went on sale in my town. I paid 39 cents for them and put one of them out on my dollar table. I sold that one to a glass expert from the museum, who had the nerve to tell me it was the oldest piece of glass I had in my shop, and asked why in the world I would sell it for only a dollar. Of course, I couldn't embarrass him by telling him I had a back-room full of them. But I did learn from that experience that many of the so-called experts have less knowledge than the average collector.

Pressed glass bowl and pitcher (cost 99 cents) and goblet (39 cents), purchased in a supermarket in 1974. (Photo by Ross Chapple)

Amber reproduction of old compote purchased in a supermarket for $1.99 in 1974. (Photo by Ross Chapple)

HISTORICAL GLASS

As with historical blue china, much of America's history can be found in its old glass. In the early 1800's, historical glass, portraying prominent persons or places, became very popular. The American Eagle adorned many plates, bowls, cups and cup plates (the tiny plates used to sit cups on while drinking from the regular saucers) sold as souvenirs at expositions and stores. Many displayed imprints of presidents and other famous personages. Almost all large cities sold souvenirs of the city in glass. I've had lacy sandwich glass plates showing buildings in New York, Chicago and San Francisco, each dated in the early 1900's.

ART GLASS

The most popular art glass was made during the Victorian era. Brides' baskets, ornate and often overlay glass of many colors, were popular wedding gifts in the late 1800's and early 1900's. Many of the fancy Victorian molds were later used for carnival or Depression glass pieces, which have become very collectible. These latter were often given as premiums by soap and cereal companies and made available by trading stamp companies.

The Sperry and Hutchinson Company sent me photo copies of their 1910, 1925-1926 catalogs, showing the beautiful cut glass that could be had for only one or two books of stamps. Much of the exquisite glass shown there has found its way into the antique shops today. I have purchased whole collections of glass from families who had obtained every piece with trading stamps. In recent years, the trading stamp companies have offered reproductions of a lot of old glass, especially carnival glass. The pieces are made in the original molds, and amateur collectors would be wise to use their trading stamps for these pieces, for they will surely become the antiques of tomorrow.

Of all the art glass, the lacy sandwich glass is by far the most desirable. The designs refract the light in such a manner that they truly look like lace. This glass was made in various colors and often in two tones. Most commonly you will find pieces which are part clear glass, part red or amber, or some other color. Sandwich glass was never made in sets, and different shades of red were the most popular. Cup plates, bowls, pitchers (usually cream pitcher sizes) may be found in most antique shops and in many auctions today, for these pieces were seldom used. Back in the 1830's the cup plates sold for as little as 4 cents each and were the most popular souvenir pieces. Next in popularity were toothpick holders, which also sold

Souvenir pitcher, dated 1904, found in thrift shop in 1974 for 50 cents. (Photo by Ross Chapple)

for only a few cents. Recently I found a tiny red and white pitcher for 50 cents in a thrift shop. It is dated 1904 and has a girl's name on it. Because this souvenir glass was more ornamental than useful, much of it has been preserved.

OPAQUE AND MILK GLASS

Opaque glass and milk glass are also popular with collectors. Many people think that if glass is white it is milk glass, but this is not necessarily so. Much of the so-called milk glass is actually opaque glass, which is older and more desirable. Opaque glass has a more translucent color, and when held to the light, the edges show a fiery red and a blue tint throughout the glass.

True milk glass has a much whiter look—a sort of dead white; no color shows through when held to the light. In the opaque pieces, often more than one color was used. Tops of covered dishes (in the shapes of rabbits, chickens, lambs, et cetera) might be shaded in tones of white, and the bottoms blue, green, or some other color. The common name for this two-tone was marble or slag, agate or cameo glass, and much of it was made between 1870 and 1880. These pieces of early opaque demand high prices on the antique market and are avidly sought. Most opaque glass was made between 1870 and 1900. Although some was made later, collectors usually use the 1900 figure as the cut-off date for good opaque glass.

STAINED GLASS

Over the past few years I've found more and more folks collecting stained glass. It has become especially popular with young people who are buying and restoring old houses. It used to be that almost anybody could find a piece of pretty stained glass from wrecking companies or junk yards, but that isn't so anymore. Old inner city homes, with their beautiful stained glass window and door panels are now falling under the wrecking machines that are destroying the art glass of a craft that reached its peak in the 13th and 14th centuries. Inflation has hit the wrecking companies, as it has every other business. John Bayless, business manager of the Washington, D.C., Cathedral, and a stained glass consultant to the Smithsonian Institution, says that wrecking companies seldom ask him to appraise stained glass, for they say they can't afford the labor expense of demolishing houses slowly, by hand, just to preserve the glass.

In addition to replacing windows and door panels and even enclosing showers with stained glass, many young collectors have discovered that hanging it on the wall with a light behind it makes it look like a stained glass window with the sun shining through. A restaurant on Capitol Hill in Washington displays old glass in this way and the effect is breathtaking.

Although old glass is vanishing from the American scene, there are a few young people now practicing the craft and making very lovely stained glass. I would buy every piece of stained glass I could find, for the price will continually go up. I suggest that those interested go into a section of the city that is to be torn down and seek out the owners of the buildings and try to buy the glass before the wrecking crews go in.

BOTTLES AND JARS

For amateurs just starting out I always suggest that they begin with bottles and jars in which everyday household products have been packaged and sold over the past twenty years or so, up to and including the present. The secret is in learning which ones to collect. Here are a few.

All the known White House Vinegar bottles and jugs from the first to present date. (Photo courtesy White House Vinegar Book)

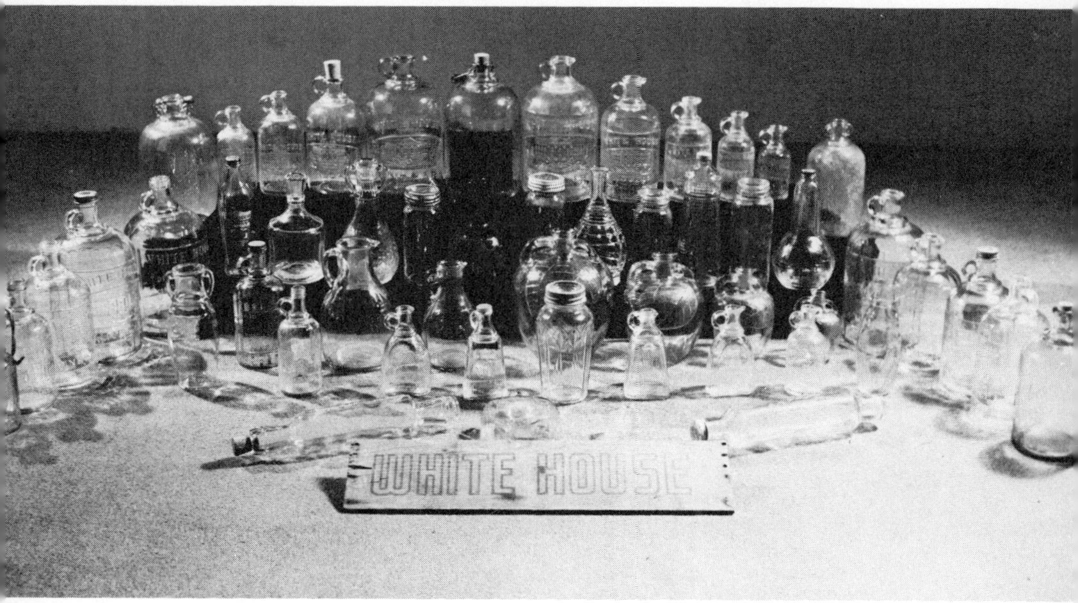

White House Vinegar Bottles

White House vinegar bottles came in many sizes and shapes and are among the hottest items sought by young collectors today. Apple-shaped vinegar jugs from the thirties bring as much as $30 or $40 for the set of four sizes. These have the apple leaf embossed on the front and also have handles. They were made in gallon, half-gallon, quart and pint sizes. The earlier jugs, from about 1923, in the same shape, with a picture of the White House embossed on the front, bring as much as $65 for the set of five. Under the picture of the White House the label reads: WHITE HOUSE BRAND VINEGAR.

This set of five White House Vinegar bottles, made from the early 1900's to the late fifties, are worth as much as $65 a set. (Photo courtesy White House Vinegar Book)

The half-pint size is the hardest to find and therefore brings the highest price. The gallon jug with wire handle and original paper label is becoming very rare. It was used in the early 1900's, and is worth $10 to $15 now.

White House vinegar jugs varied in sizes and shapes over the years, and I suggest that anyone starting to collect them should send for the *White House Vinegar Book* to Levin J. Smith Enterprises, P. O. Box 102, Independence, Virginia, 24348. This is a must for collectors and dealers, for it is the most complete book in existence on White House bottles and jugs, listing prices and is fully illustrated with photographs.

Avon Bottles and Jars

Avon bottles and jars have become very collectible in the last three or four years. It isn't unusual to see an advertisement in the daily newspapers for a garage sale listing Avon bottles for $3 to $12. Actually, there are over two thousand Avon items being collected and traded throughout the United States today. Avon was formerly the California Perfume Company, and some of the early containers from the 1900's are very valuable. Avon collectors, who number in the thousands, list the 1900 to 1930 years as "those old Avons"; 1930 to 1950 as the "middle years of Avon," and 1950 to the present as the "now years of Avon."

There are two complete books on Avon collecting. One, the *Avon Bottle Encyclopedia,* 1974-1975, by Bud Hastin, may be ordered from Bud Hastin, Box 9868, Kansas City, Missouri 64134. The other, *Avon 3,* by Joseph Weiss, may be ordered from Western World Publishers, 511 Harrison Street, San Francisco, California, 94105. Western World sponsors an Avon Club with two thousand members. You may join it by signing up for a special two-issue offer of the *Avon Quarterly* or for a full year's subscription. The *Quarterly* has pages of free ads for swapping, buying or selling Avon items, and all the latest tips on what your items are worth, their history and rarity. Any collector or would-be collector of Avon bottles can contact the author at Western World Publishers for further information. *AVON* 3 is a must for dealers and collectors alike. The fully illustrated pages will help you identify your bottles or jars and tell you exactly what they are worth.

Butterworth Syrup Bottles

On many supermarket shelves today you will find Mrs. Butterworth's syrup in bottles shaped like a woman. I not only buy them in varying sizes but I save them when they are empty—for in a very short time they may be worth as much as Log Cabin tins. Bottles of this sort make beautiful candle holders, and they look very good with other pieces of colored glass displayed on shelves in a window.

Mrs. Butterworth Syrup bottle, a collectible for the future. (Photo courtesy Lever Brothers Company)

Peanut Butter Jars

Peanut butter jars from a very few years ago are worth a great deal today. Several brands were packaged in pressed glass types of glasses and goblets; some are actual copies of old glass. You will find many of them among the antique glass displayed in shops today.

Medicine and Perfume Bottles

Medicine and perfume bottles of unusual shapes and sizes are very collectible. Colored bottles and jars are especially good. Many beginners simply collect blue, red or amber glass without regard to shape or size. Cobalt blues are the most avidly sought. I know a dealer who saves every colored bottle she can find—even the blue Phillips Milk of Magnesia and Bromo-Seltzer bottles. She keeps all the labels intact and simply stores them away for some future time when most bottles will be made of disposable plastic—or when one of the pending bills in Congress may actually pass and all glass will be required to have the date of manufacture stamped right into it. "The day such a bill passes," my friend tells me, "the collecting business will be turned upside down. Every undated piece of glass will become collectible overnight."

Wine, Whiskey and Other Old Bottles

Almost all wine bottles are collectible—even new ones. Back in the fifties when my husband and I had a shop in Pittsburgh, Pennsylvania, we found a Chianti wine bottled in a pretty decanter which sold for 99 cents. We discovered that empty bottles (minus labels) were fast sellers at $1 each. Gallon-size wine bottles make pretty lamps, and many of the tops are perfect for screw-on electrical fixtures which you may buy from most five-and-ten-cent stores.

Liquor bottles from the last ten years, worth up to $10 each. (Photo by Ross Chapple)

Whiskey bottles from five to ten years past are now selling in shops for from $2 to $5. I save every decanter-type bottle I can find, for they are increasingly popular with collectors.

Old bottles (before 1860) were usually of blown glass and have pontil marks on the bottom. The pontil mark is usually a round, rough scar in a depressed area. After 1840 many bottles were blown into two- or three-part molds, which left seams on the sides of the glass. These mold-marked seams may help indicate the approximate age of the bottle. The nearer the seams come to the top of the bottle (the mouth), the newer the bottle. Before 1860 the seams did not reach the neck; around 1880 they extended to the neckline, and around 1900 they penetrated the lip of the bottle.

I suggest that anyone seriously interested in collecting bottles send for the publication, *Collector's World Bottles and Relics,* Route 8, Box 369-A, Austin, Texas, 78703.

Fruit Jars

The name "fruit jar" was applied to canning jars as far back as 1829, possibly because fruits were the first foods successfully canned in jars. Albert Christian Revi, editor of *Spinning Wheel,* the national magazine about antiques, wrote me that as far back as the early 1950's he advised his readers to collect fruit jars. About that time they were plentiful, but today it is difficult to find them in thrift shops or at rummage sales. It is even more difficult to find them complete with their original lids of zinc (these were glass- or porcelain-lined) or glass. Mr. Revi was right—the common old canning jar used by our mothers and grandmothers has moved to the forefront of collectibles.

These green and blue jars (now discontinued), without lids, are worth $3 to $6 each. (Photo by Ross Chapple)

There are three main brands of fruit jars: Ball, Mason and Kerr. Many of the early Ball-Mason jars have the patent date, November 30, 1858, stamped into the glass. This does not mean the jar was made on that date—simply that it was patented then. I've had people try to sell me such dated jars under the impression that they were really over a hundred years old.

The prettiest jars are the colored ones. A beginner collector is safe in paying $1 or slightly more for a jar complete with lid. In the 1960's I sold most of mine for around $3 each. Since then I've seen a half-gallon blue jar sell for $12. Your best bet is to check the price they're selling for in shops and antique shows before you buy any, then never pay more than half that price.

Never pass up a separate zinc or glass clasp-on lid. A jar with a proper lid is worth much more than one without, and you can match up your lids to any lidless jars you happen to have, thus increasing their value.

GLASS COLLECTING HINTS AND TIPS

Learn to Make Small Repairs

Learn the feel of glass in your fingers. The experts can tell almost immediately from the feel if the glass is pressed or cut, or if it is old. A chipped piece of cut glass will still ring like a bell when tapped lightly, but a cracked piece will not ring at all. Never buy a piece of crystal or lead glass until you've flipped it lightly with your fingers or gently tapped it with a pencil or some other object. With cut glass it is difficult to see a crack, for it may lie in the folds of the cut.

There are experts who will grind away a chip in the glass with an electric machine; the cost is low, but this is always done at your risk. I would never tackle a deep chip, but I have often taken small nicks off the lips of goblets or glasses by slowly going over them with an emery cloth soaked in oil. You must be very careful not to scratch the glass when smoothing out the edges; the oil helps prevent this.

This can be useful to you because you'll often find a set of a pitcher and glasses, or matched goblets, and one or two will be chipped. It is almost impossible to find matching pieces and it adds a great deal to the value of your set if you can remove the chips.

Where to Buy

If you decide to collect glass of any kind, try to buy it in northern states where most is made. Collectors vacationing in the South are foolish to buy down there for chances are the dealer has purchased his glass up North and adds the expense of his trip to the price he charges you. The best thing is to take vacations or little buying trips into the states where most of the glass was originally made. Glass always sold much cheaper there, for there were no shipping charges to add to the cost, and consequently more families could afford good glass. You're much more likely to find collectible pieces in thrift shops there, too.

Originals and "Reproductions"

I read in the *Washington Post* not long ago about a glass collector who saw two toothpick holders in two different shops under the same roof. They were both reproductions by the St. Clair Glass Company, and were of the same pattern, a feather scroll of iridescent carnival glass. One dealer was asking $8 and noted that his was a copy; the other priced his at $125. The collector testified about this before a House Commerce Subcommittee investigating reproductions and forgeries in the collecting fields. They debated the legality of copying antiques without marking them as such, and as a result are now considering several bills which would make any copy "an unfair or deceptive act or practice in commerce," unless plainly marked as a reproduction.

Many collectors also advocated that all glass and china be marked with the year of manufacture although some expressed a fear that such marking would spoil the appearance of the glass. At least one maker, the St. Clair Glass Company, claimed it would not and that it would cost very little to change the date on a mold every year. Their spokesman said that they had stamped all reproductions when they first bought the company but soon had to quit because dealers refused to buy dated pieces. He believed other glass companies had the same experience, which is why they don't want to date their products—because the dealers complain. He said, "I presume these dealers are dishonest."

His company now limits reproductions to handmade glass paperweights in a design they have made for sixty years, and these are not dated although they are stamped with the company name.

Another maker, the Fenton Glass Company, complained that changing dates would be expensive and a problem for them since they make over one thousand patterns of glass. Imperial Glass Company was quick to agree, and the debate goes on. Just when the proposed bills will reach the floor of the House is anybody's guess, but it is certain that should such a bill pass, all undated glass would become collectible overnight.

Learn All You Can About Glass

If you decide to collect glass, go to the library and take out *American Glass* by George and Helen S. McKearin; all books by Ruth Webb Lee, who is one of the top authorities on American glass, and *Colored Glass of the Depression Era* by Hazel Weatherman. Visit museums and shops and study the glass first hand. Museums such as the Smithsonian in Washington have collections of old and reproduction glass. Seeing them side by side is the best way to discern the difference.

A final word: never pay big prices for any glass until you become an expert; even then it is possible to get gypped, for I don't think there is a piece of glass that hasn't been copied and it's often almost impossible to distinguish between a copy and the original.

5.

CHINA, PLATES AND POTTERY

Plate collecting ranks right along with glass, coins and stamps in popularity. In fact, it is so widespread that plate collecting clubs have sprung up all over the country, and although most of the plates collected are not old, some have become so valuable that it isn't unusual for a single plate to bring $1,000 or more though it originally cost only $25.

People collect plates of glass, ceramics, silver, copper, tin and china, but the china and fine porcelain ones are by far the most popular. When the first porcelain plates migrated from China to Europe, porcelain was so rare that it was valued more highly than gold or silver or even precious stones. It was not until the 18th century that the Germans perfected a formula for making it. Although plate collecting is not a new hobby, it is more popular these days because more plates are available to collectors. While fine porcelains can set you back a pretty penny, there are many kinds of inexpensive plates well worth collecting. Here are some of the best for amateurs to start out with.

National Capitol, Washington, D.C., platter. (Photo courtesy Smithsonian Institution)

HISTORICAL CHINA

The potteries of Staffordshire, England, had a field day in the years following the War of 1812, for they had perfected a process of decorating quite plain earthenware dishes with rich cobalt blue transfer prints which would be inexpensive to sell and highly durable. And they found a receptive and profitable market in America as well.

English pictorial scenes, as well as the pictorial record of America that unfolded on the blue and white staffordshire dishes, were done by underglaze transfer printing, using drawings, engravings and sketches produced by artists of the day.

In the early 19th century, American scenes of Niagara Falls and other picturesque landmarks such as Independence Hall in Philadelphia, churches and capitols as well as battle scenes and portraits of prominent figures adorned everything from coffee pots and tea services to mixing bowls. American buyers were caught up in a new spirit of nationalism, and the "flo-blue" or cobalt blue china became so popular that it often replaced finer china in American homes. Today you will find many pieces in historical houses all over America.

This china is very collectible and becoming harder to find at reasonable prices as the years pass. It is heavy and colorful, for the blues did not fade or wash off despite many years of use. I've recently seen collectors buy damaged pieces, for it has become so valuable that it is worth repairing. In fact I've seen repaired pieces (wired together the way professional repairers did their work in the past) sell for fantastic prices at auctions.

Tureen and lid, "Boston House." (Photo courtesy Smithsonian Institution)

Never pass up any piece of old blue china at a reasonable price, even though the design may be flowers or something other than historical places or persons. All the old blue is collectible and much in demand.

After 1830, other colors began to appear on the historical china, but none was ever so popular as the cobalt blue. There are pinks, pale blues and all shades of browns. Although they are collectible, they are not as valuable as the blues.

When you speak of "historical china," dealers and collectors alike immediately think you mean only the hundred-year-old pieces, but I feel inclined to include any of the reproductions that portray a part of American life, past or present, as well. There are pretty souvenir pieces being sold today in cobalt blues, portraying presidents or historical scenes. This china is lighter in weight and not comparable to the old Staffordshire, but it is certainly collectible too.

Martha Washington plate, from the Haviland reissues of Presidential china sold through various plate companies after 1969. (Photo courtesy Haviland China Company)

Mary Todd Lincoln plate, from the Haviland reissues of Presidential china. (Photo courtesy Haviland China Company)

REISSUES OF PRESIDENTIAL CHINA

Haviland and Company, Limoges, France—one of the oldest and most famous china companies in the world—created special fine china services for several of our First Ladies in the White House, beginning as far back as Martha Washington, and reflecting their personal tastes. In 1969, the Haviland Company began making reissues of their Presidential china. These elegant copies are unique in the field of collecting, and many patterns are still available.

The first commemorative plate in this Presidential reissue was the Martha Washington, an 8½-inch plate in her chosen pattern, showing the fifteen states of the Union linked in chain fashion around the border. It was first reissued in 1876, to celebrate the Centenary of the Declaration of Independence.

Mary Todd Lincoln personally selected her pattern from Haviland in 1861. The center of each plate portrays an eagle, wings outstretched, atop the National Shield, seemingly passing from dark clouds into bright sunshine. The deep purple border is encircled with two entwined hand-applied gold cables representing the unification of the North and South.

Grant "Flower Set" plate from Haviland reissues of Presidential china of Mrs. Grant's plate. (Photo courtesy Haviland China Company)

Almost every flower native to our country was used in decorating the Grant China, known as the "Flower Set." The reissue plate used the center flower, a rose, that has at least twenty-one different color changes in it. The plate is scalloped, with the Seal set in the border.

The Hayes China that caused the uproar when it was sold at auction was first produced by Haviland in 1880. Mrs. Hayes chose an American designer, and her plates show fruits, vegetables, flowers, game, fish and flowers native to America. In fact her china had more color and flair than any other presidential china I've seen.

Plate from Mrs. Rutherford B. Hayes china from Haviland reissues of Presidential china. (Photo courtesy Haviland China Company)

Spice cabinet used for miniature china set, total cost less than 50 cents. (Photo by Ross Chapple)

If you're interested in getting details on how to obtain reissues of the Presidential China, I suggest you write to Haviland and Company, 11 East 26th Street, New York City.

MINIATURE CHINA

Recently, I started a collection of children's miniature tea sets. I found about twenty pieces at a rummage sale for 50 cents. Included are parts of three sets, all china. Then I found a beat-up spice shelf for 10 cents at another sale, and put together a miniature wall china closet. The whole thing cost me less than 50 cents, for I still have enough pieces of the tea sets to fill another shelf, when I find one. I found a cream pitcher and six tiny cups and saucers for $3 at another thrift shop. They are real Meissen, and each piece is marked with the crossed swords of the Meissen mark.

LIMITED EDITIONS

Bing and Grondahl of Denmark produced their first dated annual plate back in 1895 and have produced one every year since. That 1895 plate, which brought 50 cents on the open market, is worth $2,700 today.

Each year quality china companies around the world produce a limited number of chosen plates and then destroy the molds. Demand for these limited editions, sold via mail by several famous plate houses, far exceeds the supplies and most of them sell out, raising values substantially. Within a year or two, they often join the "rare plate lists," selling for as much as 500% above their original prices.

Norman Rockwell "Streaker" plate, which first appeared on the cover of the Saturday Evening Post *back in 1921. (Photo courtesy Joy's Limited)*

PORTRAIT, COMMEMORATIVE AND ADVERTISING PLATES

Portrait, commemorative and advertising plates are always popular items to collect. In Pittsburgh I bought ten old porcelain plates with the name of a local store on them. They were not pretty, for their portraits of pretty women had been marred with time, but the name of the local store was still very clear. I paid only 25 cents a piece for them so I put them on my dollar table and one customer bought the entire set. A week or so later that store advertised, via radio and newspaper, offering to pay $50 per plate for any one of them—for they had given them out on their opening fifty years before. As you see, this was another of my unlucky sales—you just never know when some advertising item like that may be recalled for a lot more than its intrinsic worth.

I once had a customer in Pittsburgh who collected only portrait plates and it didn't matter to her whose portraits they were. She had plates with Indian, historical figures, children, chorus girls, movie stars and just about anybody else you could think of. In her large, old-fashioned house she displayed them on built-in plate racks around the walls of the hall, kitchen and dining room. She told me she had started collecting twenty-six years earlier when she had first seen her house. The plate racks were all there then, except that they were empty, but for twenty-two plates which were the prettiest she'd ever seen—handpainted portrait plates of beautiful, old-fashioned girls, which she still had on display in the dining room, and in fact that's why she bought the house. She told her husband then that she was going to fill every bit of wall space with plates, and it scared the daylights out of him. All the same, she did it—for all those twenty-six years, she traded fancy work, tended babies, and did odd jobs for folks in exchange for her plates. She was known around town as the "portrait plate lady," and it helped, for hardly a week went by that she didn't get calls from strangers with plates to trade.

"But," she told me, "I haven't got room for any more; I've done what I set out to do—my racks are filled."

This conversation took place some years ago, and I often wonder whatever happened to my portrait plate lady. Of one thing I'm very sure—her collection is worth a fortune today.

AMERICAN POTTERY

Very little of our earliest American Indian pottery has been discovered in good condition, because it was made of reddish clay (similar to brick), and was far less durable than later forms. Indian pots of this red clay have been unearthed by archaeologists during excavations, but seldom were the pieces intact. The basic color of this redware was derived from traces of iron oxide in the clay. Frequently the potters used a pure form of lead glaze (which is actually glass) in finishing the pieces, thus retaining the original redness.

There are few records of the earliest American potters, but pottery is known to have been made here as early as 1625 in Jamestown, Virginia. In the colonies, families made their own crude pottery in the kitchens or dairy sheds. Many flower pots we buy today are made from a more refined process of the same red clay pottery. In Pennsylvania, the Dutch decorated their redware with fancy designs, and although redware fell from favor after the introduction of stoneware, many Pennsylvania families continued to make it, and many of their decorated pieces are still found today.

Stoneware (which is very collectible) was developed by a German potter in the 1400's. He discovered that by firing certain types of clay at high temperature he could produce a hard, waterproof pottery. A few of the colonists brought the know-how with them to America; the best known were the Bell family in the Shenandoah Valley of Virginia. Peter Bell, the founder, worked in Virginia and Maryland from 1800 to 1845. His sons and daughters carried on his work and their last pottery in Strasburg, Virginia, was closed in 1908.

Glazing was simply done by throwing a quantity of salt into the kiln during firing, thus depositing a thin coat of glaze over the pottery. Churns, crocks, jugs and many other pieces of kitchenware were made of this gray stoneware. Many were painted in cobalt blue (these are the most desirable to collect) or scratched with the blue. Most decorated stoneware was marked by the potters, which makes it easier to ascertain the ages of these pieces.

Stoneware was perhaps the most essential of all colonial wares. Milk was put to cool in springs and wells in stoneware jugs; whiskey and water were stored in them; food was baked or warmed over in stoneware plates. Stoneware was easily cleaned, completely waterproof and although heavy kept things cool or hot longer than pewter or wood.

Because much of the stoneware is not pretty, it is easier to find than almost any other collectible ware. Frequently you will find jugs (with corncob stoppers) for $3 or less, and churns for up to about $10. These old churns make lovely umbrella stands or vases for long-stemmed flowers or shrubs.

Stoneware salt boxes are much in demand. These were made with open holes in the back for hanging on the wall and usually had hinged wooden tops. Salt boxes hung over almost every kitchen stove and many people collect them. Should you find one without the lid, buy it, for the lids can be replaced.

CROCKERY JARS

Many imported cheeses come in crockery type jars that are not only collectible for the future but may be found in most antique shops today. It is almost impossible to tell some of them from the old apple butter jars that grandma used. Even the lids are fastened in the same way, with heavy wire clasps.

Learn to distinguish the old stoneware from ceramics of today. Old pieces were usually less perfect, heavier, and unfinished (unglazed) on the bottoms. When you've collected pottery for a while, you will learn to tell the old from the new by the bottoms—a piece in use for a long time becomes worn there, and almost all stoneware was made for use rather than for decorative purposes, as much china was.

One word of advice—whatever you're collecting, never pass up a lid or a single cup or saucer. I always buy lids of every description, for a coffee or tea pot isn't worth much if the lid is missing, and that one small piece is worth a lot of money to a dealer with a lidless piece. That goes for tureen lids too.

Here are some of the better-known plate dealers and clubs:

Joy's Limited Editions, Merchandise Mart Plaza, Chicago, Illinois 60654, sends out a monthly news letter to all its members, showing the latest pictures of collector plates with details such as quantity produced, sizes of plates, background of producers, invest-

The Lafayette Legacy plate, 1776-1976 by Restieau, a first edition of genuine D'Arceau-Limoges Fine Art collector's plate. (Photo courtesy Bradford Galleries)

ment potential (including rumors they hear from dozens of other dealers around the country on the demand and popularity of various collector plates). The increase in value of these plates is well illustrated by the 1969 Bing and Grondahl's Mother's Day plate, which Joy's Limited sold for $9 and will now buy back for $189 (although Joy claims that some of her competitors get up to $375 each for them). A letter to Joy will bring details on how to join the club.

Bradford Galleries Exchange, 1000 Sunset Ridge Road, Northbrook, Illinois 60662, is another of the world's principal plate exchanges, serving more than a quarter million collectors. On request, they will send you a brochure on their plates, including the Lafayette Legacy 1776-1976—French Limoges plates being sold in America for the first time in three centuries. Also available is their current market report, an eight-point checklist for market evaluations of collector's plates.

Wedgwood Collector's Society, 555 Madison Avenue, New York, New York 10022, offers for $7 a complimentary plaque and membership in this popular club. Members receive newsletters listing Wedgwood Special Edition plates and other collectibles. Each is designed expressly for the society and carries the exclusive society backstamp and a likeness of Josiah Wedgwood, founder of the two-hundred-year-old English Wedgwood Company.

Armstrong's, 150 East Third Street, Pomona, California 91766 is the largest plate dealer on the West Coast. They carry not only a large selection of collector's plates, but also one of the largest selections of porcelain sculpture in the United States. They do a tremendous mail-order business with collectors in every state in the Union. Beautiful brochures will be sent on request, with complete price listings, and they deliver anywhere in the country at no additional cost, with items fully insured.

There are many other clubs in the plate field and most of them advertise from time to time in national women's magazines and newspapers. I suggest that any time you see an advertisement, write for details if you're interested in plate collecting. From all recent indications, this is one of the most profitable hobbies to have.

6.

COINS

"It's hard to think of anything more tangible that will reach more people and put more history into their hands than a coin. Art, science, economics—these, too, are reflected in coins." These were the opening words of a talk given by the Honorable Mary T. Brooks, Director of the Mint. Mrs. Brooks was right, for coins are the one item in our lives that pass through the hands of all people, young and old, rich or poor. Coins are available to all of us, to be spent, saved or collected.

Since this book is being written for amateurs, we'll assume that coin collecting will be done on a beginner's scale—which means starting out with the everyday coins that come into your pocket. Your ordinary change—especially pennies—can harbor unsuspected treasures, if you know how to look for them. But going into it seriously—buying rare coins for collecting can be an expensive and dangerous business for the amateur. True, for the past five to ten years the prices of rare coins have been rising steadily, but one never knows when the bottom may fall out and collectors (especially those buying for metal content rather than numismatic value) may stand to lose most of their investment. As in the stock market, the value of coins fluctuates with economic conditions.

There are a number of things that make ordinary coins valuable. Age and rarity, of course—an old coin is likely to be less available (hence more valuable) than a new one; some issues were struck in small quantities to start with.

There are also errors, some famous, some unknown, that keep cropping up, that greatly increase the value of a coin. Error coins turn up in unexpected places—in the Mint's own penny bags, for instance. (These are small copies of bags used by the Mint to transport coins to Federal Reserve banks, and they contain 15 pennies (five from each of the three Mints) of a given year.) A few years ago, there were news reports of a man who ordered 25 of the 1972 bags, only to find an odd-looking coin in one of them: a penny struck on a dime planchet (coin blank). Since it bore the "S" (San Francisco) Mint mark, and since San Francisco had struck only proof dimes in 1972, it had to be a proof planchet. The usual price for a penny struck in error on a dime planchet is about $65, but only one other penny on a proof dime planchet is known—a 1968S—so the 1972 find is estimated to be worth $500. That man's 25 minibags cost $8; at 15 pennies per bag, his error coin cost him a little over 2 cents.

Since the penny shortage in 1974, penny bags have not been made available to the public; however, coins in proof sets may be ordered by mail from the Bureau of the Mint, 55 Mint Street, San Francisco, California, 94175. Since prices on proof sets tend to fluctuate, it is wise to write the Mint for a current price list.

A coin's history can also greatly influence its value. Take, for instance, the coin secreted on board the Gemini 7 spacecraft in 1965. The coin was pretty valuable already—a 1793 large penny normally worth about $2,000. After its journey in space it was sold for $15,000, and its value is now estimated at close to $100,000.

One warning is in order: the director of the American Numismatic Association's coin certification service says that collectors spend more than one million dollars a year on bogus coins. Most of the counterfeiting operations have been found in the Middle East.

In 1970, a Malaysian outfit flooded the United States with 3,000 phony "pieces of eight" which sold to unsuspecting collectors for $50 each, mostly through mail order advertisements. More recently, in 1973, the Treasury Department began an investigation into a Connecticut company which sent out direct mail advertisements for facsimiles of antique coins. The advertisements claimed they were perfect reproductions of the originals and nowhere indicated that they were marked as copies.

There is a bill now before Congress to protect collectors of antique coins and political memorabilia from counterfeiters. Under its provisions any copy of a coin, paper money or token commemorative medal made in the United States or imported into this country must be marked *copy*.

This is another danger area. Often you may find a coin that appears to you to be in fine or extra fine condition only to have a dealer tell you that the condition is only good. There is a great difference in value between the various conditions. All the experts urge collectors to be extremely careful in this area, for it's difficult to establish the grade of a coin with any degree of accuracy, and a mistake can be costly. Unless you are a seasoned collector, you should not be your own final authority: always get professional advice. And, as in all dealings in old and rare things, *deal only with reputable dealers.*

Here, to give you an idea, are photographs, front and back, of an extra fine wheat penny. Compare your own pennies to these photographs to determine if they, too, are extra fine, or in any of the following conditions:

PROOF: Faces of coins have mirror-like surfaces. A proof coin is a specially struck coin with extra-sharp detail and brilliant finish. These are offered directly to collectors through special mail order at slightly higher prices. Before 1965, proofs were struck only in Philadelphia. Since then, in San Francisco.

UNCIRCULATED: Almost perfect condition. Shiny, mirror-like surface.

Extra fine: Some high spots beginning to show wear. Luster still shows.

Very fine: Obvious wear on high spots. Some luster remaining. Cheek and jawbone slightly flattened.

Fine: Circulated but with very little wear. Wheat stalk ends show signs of wear.

Very good: Letters and designs are clearly defined. Half of wheat stalk ends are worn off. Leaves show wear.

Good: Coin may show considerable wear but all mottoes and designs show clearly. Coin must have full rim on both sides. All details of wheat stalk ends are gone.

The history of the lowly copper penny is as old as the history of our country. In 1785, when Congress adopted the monetary system proposed by Thomas Jefferson providing the dollar as our principal monetary unit, it provided for copper coins one two-hundredth of the value of a dollar. A year later it authorized the minting of copper

Face side of wheat penny, 1909.

coins valuing one-hundredth of a dollar. These were respectively called half-cents and cents, and both continued in use until the half-cent was discontinued in 1857. Three-cent and two-cent pieces were briefly minted during the 19th century, but the cent, or penny, is the one that has proved durable up through our present time.

The form of the modern cent, composed of 95% copper and 5% tin and zinc, dates from 1864. However, during World War II, to conserve the supply of copper, the cent was made of zinc-coated steel. The copper content was restored in 1944, and a final change in 1962 stabilized the alloy at 95% copper and 5% zinc.

You may think that one penny looks much like another, but there have been several changes in style and these are important to collectors as they affect the value—the Lincoln wheat penny and the Indian Head are two to watch out for. The Lincoln penny, which made its initial appearance in 1909, marked a radical departure from accepted styling, introducing as it did a portrait coin in the regular series. A strong feeling had always prevailed against using portraits on our coins but public sentiment on the 100th anniversary of Lincoln's birth overcame the old prejudice. In addition to prescribed elements for U.S. coins—*Liberty* and the date—the motto IN GOD WE TRUST appeared for the first time on a coin of this denomination. In fact Congress had authorized the use of this expression on our coins during Lincoln's term of office. The reverse of the coin has a very simple design bearing two heads of wheat in memorial style. Between these, in the center, are the denomination and UNITED STATES OF AMERICA, while curving around the upper border is the national motto, E PLURIBUS UNUM. The initials of the designer, Victor David Brenner, appeared on the original issue, but people protested that they were too conspicuous and detracted from the design. In future issues the initials were eliminated, but they were restored in 1918, and are to be found in minute form on the rim, just under Lincoln's shoulder.

More pennies are produced than any other denomination, which makes the Lincoln piece a familiar item on the national scene. In

Reverse side of wheat penny.

1959 the design was revised in celebration of the 150th anniversary of Lincoln's birth. This time the reverse shows the Lincoln Memorial in Washington as the central motif; the legends E PLURIBUS UNUM and UNITED STATES OF AMERICA form the rest of the design, together with the denomination. The designer's initials, FG, appear on the right, near the shrubbery.

When I was a child, Indian Head pennies were also plentiful. Many a time I went to the candy store with them to buy penny candy. My mother used to save many that she found in her change as she marketed for the family. Of course, there was no such thing as sales tax in those days, and we didn't get as many pennies in our change as we do today. My sister has about thirty or forty dollars in Indian Head pennies today, and although they may be worth triple their face value, I doubt she has more than a few rare ones.

Today, I save all the Lincoln pennies I can find of that first design, from 1909 to 1959, with the heads of wheat on the back. In a few years, they will compare to the Indian Head in scarcity and value. Then too there are a few rare pennies among the wheat pennies, and it's fun looking for them.

In the recent United States Coin Catalog, put out by Gene Hessler, Curator of the Chase Manhattan Bank Money Museum, and Don Hirschhorn, the following Lincoln "wheat" pennies are listed as most valuable:

> The letters ADP beside certain coins listed here means *average dealer price*. This means the average dealer in this country will most likely pay that price for such a coin.

1909: from 15¢ (good condition) to $75 (proof)
1909: VDB from 60 ¢ (good) to $275 (proof)
1909 S: from $10 (ADP) to $55 (uncirculated)
1910: from 10¢ (good) to $85 (proof)
1910 S: from $1 (ADP) to $35 (uncirculated)
1911: from 10¢ (good) to $85 (uncirculated)
1911 D: from 50¢ (ADP) to $25 (uncirculated)
1911 S: from $2.50 (ADP) to $45 (uncirculated)
1912: from 10¢ (good) to $90 (proof)
1912 D: from 50¢ (ADP) to $40 (uncirculated)
1913: from 10¢ (good) to $90 (proof)
1913 D: from 65¢ (good) to $35 (uncirculated)
1913 S: from $1 (ADP) to $35 (uncirculated)
1914: from 15¢ (good) to $150 (proof)
1914 D: from $18 (ADP) to $485 (uncirculated)
1914 S: from $1.25 (ADP) to $55 (uncirculated)
1915: from 35¢ (good) to $225 (proof)
1915 D: from 30¢ (good) to $20 (uncirculated)
1915 S: from $1 (ADP) to $40 (uncirculated)
1916: from 10¢ (good) to $7 (uncirculated)
1916 D: from 15¢ (good) to $18.75 (uncirculated)
1916 S: from 30¢ (good) to $20 (uncirculated)
1917: from 10¢ (good) to $6 (uncirculated)
1917 D: from 15¢ (good) to $22.50 (uncirculated)
1917 S: from 15¢ (good) to $25 (uncirculated)

1918: from 10¢ (good) to $7.50 (uncirculated)
1918 D: from 15¢ (good) to $27.50 (uncirculated)
1918 S: from 15¢ (good) to $30 (uncirculated)
1919: from 10¢ (good) to $6 (uncirculated)
1919 D: from 15¢ (good) to $15 (uncirculated)
1919 S: from 10¢ (good) to $15 (uncirculated)
1920: from 10¢ (good) to $5.50 (uncirculated)
1920 D: from 15¢ (good) to $30 (uncirculated)
1920 S: from 10¢ (good) to $27.50 (uncirculated)
1921: from 10¢ (good) to $16 (uncirculated)
1921 S: from 35¢ (good) to $125 (uncirculated)
1922: from $20 (ADP) to $750 (uncirculated)
1922 D: from $1 (ADP) to $40 (uncirculated)
1923: from 10¢ (good) to $6.75 (uncirculated)
1923 S: from 65¢ (good) to $215 (uncirculated)
1924: from 10¢ (good) to $12.50 (uncirculated)
1924 D: from $3 (ADP) to $165 (uncirculated)
1924 S: from 35¢ (good) to $85 (uncirculated)
1925: from 10¢ (good) to $5.75 (uncirculated)
1925 D: from 15¢ (good) to $25 (uncirculated)
1925 S: from 15¢ (good) to $27.50 (uncirculated)

The most valuable cent in the rest of this series is the 1931 S, which is listed at from $12 (ADP) to $40 uncirculated. If you are collecting, it is important to buy the new coin catalogs each year, for the values do change.

One last note on pennies: early in 1974, speculators began clamoring for the new 1974 S pennies, offering as high as $475 for a $50 bag. When other speculators upped that price to as much as $900 per $50 bag, an embargo was placed on all the coins from the San Francisco Mint, except for a mail order allowance for collectors. Even that was cancelled, however, and the Mint announced that in order to make certain that these much sought after coins would be widely distributed, the Federal Reserve would mix the S cents in with other cents they distributed to banks.

There was certainly a shortage of pennies in 1974, and it created quite a stir throughout the country. The price of copper was up, and

I know of one manufacturing company that found it cheaper to punch a hole in a copper cent than to make a washer needed for a machine—the washer would have cost a cent and a half. Banks everywhere advertised to buy pennies at $1.10 to $1.25 a hundred. Hoarders did let go of millions of their coppers at a terrific profit, but when the banks limited their generous offers shortly thereafter, pennies vanished from the marketplace again. It wasn't unusual to see signs posted in grocery stores declaring their need for pennies, and at least one department store in North Carolina began giving out sticks of candy in lieu of pennies in change, until the thing backfired and customers began bringing in the sticks of candy to pay for their purchases. Rumors (and the Mint declares they are only rumors) began to circulate that within a few years the penny may no longer be minted at all.

Kennedy memorial half dollar minted in 1964.

However that may be, it seems to me at this point that if coin speculators are so eager to buy up these 1974 S cents, they must be very collectible. If you should happen to find them in your change, by all means hold on to them.

All our other coins have their rarities and special issues (like the Kennedy memorial half-dollar), and you'll find them listed in current coin catalogs. But the other coin of special interest (to me, at least) is the silver dollar. Silver dollars command such a premium today that the variety and condition are of secondary interest to collectors. The first silver dollars were authorized in April 1792 and appeared two years later. Those first 1794 coins were of two types—with two or with three leaves beneath each wing of the eagle on the reverse, and there were eleven variants of the two-leaf type. Other, later, variants included large and small dates; ten, thirteen and fifteen stars on the reverse; four or five berries or no berries; large, small or medium berries.

One of the most publicized and valuable is the 1804 silver dollar, which authorities believe was actually struck between 1834 and 1835, and then in presentation proof sets only. Restrikes were made in 1859 to satisfy certain collectors, but only seven known pieces have been adjudged as genuine. Only eight of the "original" 1804 silver dollars are known and as far back as twenty years ago brought in over $10,000. About ten years ago they brought in $28,000 and $29,000, which shows you how much their value has increased in recent years.

Throughout the 19th century and up to the present time, silver dollar production has been on-again, off-again, as Congress has revised their metal content or, in certain years, failed to authorize their production altogether. There have been a number of curious episodes, as for example in 1918, when the Government melted down over 270 million silver dollars, virtually all for export to India. Production began again in 1921, continued through 1928, then halted. It was resumed in 1934 and 1935, then there followed thirty-six silver-dollarless years before the Eisenhower dollar came out in 1971.

Eisenhower dollar.

Since then there has been much in the newspapers about the Ike dollar. After August 1973 commercial banks, except in a few areas, stopped handling them, and with the Federal Reserve pipelines clogged with 1971 and 1972 coins, the Mint decided not to strike any 1973 dollars for circulation. The only 1973 Ike dollars available are those in proof and uncirculated sets and these are no longer available to collectors from the Mint, orders having been cut off in January 1973 for proof sets, and in April 1973 for uncirculated sets.

If you follow my advice, you'll hold on to any silver dollar you find. Although I don't specialize in coin collecting, I do keep an eagle eye on all the coins around me. Recently at a grocery store checkout counter I stood beside a woman who extended an old 1892 silver dollar to pay for bread and cheese. She was pleased when I offered to buy it for $2—and it was a good buy for me, for that dollar is listed at $5 in the coin catalog.

New bicentennial quarter minted in 1975.

For the future, all collectors should note the drastic changes taking place in American coinage in 1975, which are bound to have far-reaching effects. From July 4, 1975 to January 1, 1977, all the new Bicentennial coins making their appearance in the marketplaces and all the dollars, half-dollars and quarters minted for issuance will bear the dates 1776-1976, instead of the actual date of coinage. Unless I am very mistaken, the dated coins of previous years will begin to disappear from the marketplace and every dated coin will increase in value. We all saw what happened when we changed from silver- to copper-clad coins—within months the all-silver dimes, quarters, halves and silver dollars disappeared from daily change, only to reappear in coin shops for several times their monetary value.

The Mint expects to strike 1.4 billion quarters, 400 million half-dollars and 225 million dollars to meet commercial demand for the new circulating Bicentennial coins. In addition, at least 45 million 40% silver-clad proof and uncirculated specimens of the new coins will be struck for sale to the public. Those wishing to receive information and to be put on the mailing lists for ordering should write: The Bureau of the Mint, 55 Mint Street, San Francisco, California 94175.

My advice to beginner collectors of coins is this: buy the latest coin catalog; subscribe to one of the very good coin publications, such as *Numismatic News,* Coin Collector's Capital, Iola, Wisconsin 54945; *Numismatic Scrapbook Magazine,* P. O. Box 150, Sidney, Ohio 45365, or to any of the other fine coin publications.

New bicentennial half dollar minted in 1975.

New bicentennial dollar minted in 1975.

Buy only proof or uncirculated coins directly from the Mint and, when you find a regular antique shop that sells coins too, learn to trade other antique items for coins. Old coins do find their way into the marketplace once in a great while and you'll see them if you look out, just as I acquired my 1892 silver dollar. Keep your eyes open, and if you really enjoy looking for coins remember you'll seldom find them in rolls from the bank, for coins turned in to the banks are already culled for old ones. In principle, never hand a clerk $1.02 for a purchase, if you have two single dollar bills—your 98 cents in change may contain a prize you may never find anywhere again.

7.

BOOKS

Books are ideal collectibles for amateurs on a shoestring budget—they're everywhere. There is a greater chance of finding a rare book than almost any other collectible item. Auctions, attics, barns, thrift shops, garage and basement sales always have some books. Even in second-hand book stores it's possible to uncover a real find, for unless the dealer keeps up on the current market trends, it's difficult for him to spot something rare or know its value. Besides, many dealers buy in bulk, and do not bother to look up every book in the lot.

If you're collecting books, your investment will be small. I'm speaking for the beginner, who will be looking for his rarities in out-of-the-way places. However, there are certain rules to follow. Never, never ask a dealer if he has a particular rare book you're hoping to find. Once I sold a rare copy of one of Walt Whitman's books to a dealer, along with several boxes of miscellaneous books. Quite by accident I discovered its value, and when I went back to ask him where he had put it, he was immediately suspicious. Keeping a poker face is not one of my talents, and when I asked to buy it back he looked it up in a catalog. He then thanked me for calling his attention to it, and of course he kept it.

Not all old books are rare. Many people think that because a book was published a hundred years ago, it must be worth a lot of money. This isn't necessarily so. I've had customers who expected me to pay huge sums for old books that were not worth anything to me. The best thing about finding a very old book is that it may turn up a letter or autograph that is worth a great deal. A few years ago, a couple from Arlington, Virginia, went on an antique junket through southern Virginia. She collected glass and he was interested in books. In a little antique shop one day he bought two books for 50 cents each. One was *United States Secret Service in the Late War* (1897) and the other, *The Life of Jefferson Davis* (1868). He was pleased enough but when he got home and examined his books more closely, several envelopes spilled out of one of them.

On the back of one of the envelopes, he spotted the signature "A. Lincoln." The letter inside was from a Levi Davis of Illinois to President Lincoln, asking to be appointed Lieutenant in the Union Army. Lincoln's handwriting on the back of the envelope read: *If the Secretary of War knows no objection except that he is a relative of his, let him be appointed on my responsibility. May 13, 1862.*

One of the other letters was from General Ulysses S. Grant. Dr. Percy Powell of the Library of Congress Division of Manuscripts—and a prominent authority on Lincoln and Grant signatures—attested to their authenticity, saying that most any Lincoln indorsement would bring $100 or $200 each. He also said he'd like to have a chance to acquire them for the Library of Congress.

So if you come across old letters or signatures you believe are those of famous people, the Library of Congress Division of Manuscripts is the place to send them for authentication.

There are two books essential to serious book collectors: *Gold in Your Attic* by Van Allen Bradley, published by Fleet Press, New York, and his later book, *Handbook of Values,* published by G. P. Putnam's Sons, New York. If you can't afford to buy them at the outset, you can find them in your library. If they are in the reference section and can't be borrowed, spend an hour or two each week copying onto file cards the rare or valuable books listed there. Many rare books do not say *first edition* or have identifying marks on the title page or elsewhere in front. Mr. Bradley tells you explicitly how to identify rare editions (often by misprints on certain pages or some differences in various editions).

Set up a filing system, listing books (one to a card) by title, cross-filing on a separate card under the author's name. On this card, put all pertinent information—how to identify the book; its worth (the listed price is what the book has already brought at auction and you won't necessarily get that much unless you find a buyer willing to pay retail price for it); publisher and year of publication. You will learn more by copying for your files than you ever will by just reading, and then, too, you'll have all the information at your fingertips. I keep such a file on my desk so that when I happen across a book when I'm on a buying trip and think it may be rare, I call home and have my family look it up for me. If the filing system is kept simple, anyone can look things up for you in just a moment.

Here are a few examples from my files:

MOBY DICK OR THE WHALE Herman Melville
Harper & Bros. Publisher London
1851 Richard Bently
$2,500

BEN HUR A Tale of the Christ by Lew Wallace
Franklin Squire New York Harper & Bros.
1st edition dedication: "To the wife of my youth"
$250

LITTLE WOMEN 2 volumes Louisa M. Alcott
Boston 1868-1869
Vol. 1 lacking "Part I" at base of spine.
Vol. 2 no notice of little women.

ALICE'S [on first line]
ADVENTURES IN WONDERLAND [2nd line]
Lewis Carroll with 42 illustrations by John Tenniel
D. Appleton & Co. 445 Broadway, New York 1886
$500 good; $175 worn

THE MODERN ART OF TAMING WILD HORSES
by J. S. Rarey
Printed by the State Journal
Columbus County 1856
$350.

THE MORMON WAY–BILL
Salt Lake City 1832 Joseph Cain's & Arieh Brower's
$3,400

Note that anything "Mormon" is very valuable if published at the beginning of the movement West. The *Latter Day Saint's Emigrants Guide* by Brigham Young, St. Louis, 1848, is worth over $2,000.

There are so many valuable books to be found that it would take several volumes to list them all. All county and state histories are valuable; so are guide books, animal and bird books (*Birds of America* by Audubon in seven volumes is worth over $1,000 in good condition), old cook books, many old medical books, travel books and books relating personal experiences in early history. A woman I know who owns over five thousand cookbooks believes that regional cookbooks will be real collector's items of the future.

Classified sections of antiques magazines and newspapers have pages of books wanted, some by individuals and many by rare book shops. *Never* send a book out in response to an advertisement, no matter where you see it. Always write first and describe the book you have for sale. Describe it honestly—if it's worn, say so, and name your price. Then wait until you have a commitment from the advertiser. Then insure the book, mail it and wait a reasonable time for reply.

If you want to make inquiries, here are a few reliable rare book dealers:

Carnegie Book Shop
140 E. 59th Street
New York, New York 10022

Philip C. Durchnes
699 Madison Avenue
New York, New York 10021

House of Books, Limited
667 Madison Avenue
New York, New York 10021

Maxwell Hunley
9533 Santa Monica Boulevard
Beverly Hills, California 90213

Other rare book dealers are listed in *Gold in Your Attic*. The book section of your Sunday paper also lists dealers in your own locality as well as those who do mail order business.

Remember that it is possible to come across old or rare books that are not listed. Recently, at a rummage sale, I bought a book in Italian, dated 1714. It cost me 50 cents and it is in perfect condition, although I cannot read a word of it. The only thing I can understand are the dates printed on each page. I have since discovered that it is a record of Catholic priests ordained from 1300 through 1700. Obviously this is a book that should interest the Catholic Church, and I intend to take it to the Catholic University, for it will be more important and therefore worth more to a Catholic library than to

1714 book bought at rummage sale, for 50 cents. (Photo by Ross Chapple)

any rare book store. This applies to books on any religion, organizations such as Masons, or books containing county or state histories. Contact the organization or state or county concerned—they all have archives and libraries eager to obtain rare books and documents.

When trying to sell books you don't want, remember that dealers must make a profit and will normally pay half the going market price. Often books remain on shelves for a long time before the right collector comes along. I've found the best way to sell books of above-average value is to collect several different kinds, and then advertise a collection of one specific category at a time. Or if you have many not-so-rare though collectible books, check their prices in some of the guides I've mentioned (or others in your library), and have a house sale on books alone, pricing them at about two-thirds of the prices you find listed. These not-so-rare books that are merely out of print will not make you rich, but they'll keep you in spending money while you're looking for the great rarity you may find in your neighbor's attic or in the thrift shop just around the corner. There's money to be made in books, and as I started by saying, the nice thing is that you don't have to have a fortune to invest—you don't need a truck to transport them and they're literally everywhere you go.

8.

MAGAZINES, COMIC BOOKS AND PAMPHLETS

Would you believe that the first issue of *Playboy* magazine (November, 1953) is listed at from $150 to $200 in a collector's price guide? Not only that—the January 1954 issue is listed at $45, the February 1954 issue at $40, and all the 1954 issues at $25 each. The January 1955 issue lists at $15, and all others of that year at $12.50. All 1956 issues are $8.50; 1957 issues are $7; 1958's at $6.50; 1959's at $5.50; 1960's at $4.75; 1961's at $4, and so on, up through 1966.

When Hugh Hefner started publishing *Playboy* in 1953, financed by his entire bankroll of $600, he put out 70,000 copies of that first edition, with a picture of Marilyn Monroe on the cover and a centerfold of her in the nude. It was undated and put together by hand by Mr. Hefner and his associates. Fifty-one thousand copies were sold. Nobody seems to know what happened to the other 19,000 copies, but should someone find them, they'd stumble onto a small fortune.

The first issues of almost any magazine are worth something, especially if that magazine has folded. I haven't any first issues, but would buy them if I came across them in a second-hand shop. However, I have saved the last issues of *Saturday Evening Post, Life* and *Look* magazines—someday they too will be collectible, along with many other of their issues.

Mad magazine (which began with Number 24, as the first 23 issues were comic books) is becoming collectible. The first issue (number 24) is listed at $12.50 in the price guide; the next at $10, and each issue after that at about $1.

Almost all science fiction and horror comics are collectible. The old Buck Rogers comics continue to rise in value. In the last few years, many detective and adventure comics such as Dick Tracy and Superman have joined the ranks. A *Dick Tracy Secret Detective Method and Magic Tricks* booklet, given away free for a box top by Quaker Oats Company a few years back, is worth $35 today. *Captain Marvel's Magic Eyes,* which sold for 10 cents, is now valued at $5.

Pamphlets of all sorts from olden times have become very rare and quite valuable. Perhaps this is because so many were thrown away as useless junk, as we do our fourth-class mail today. I will list a few and the prices they've brought at auction to show you that you should never skip over a paper or a booklet until you find out what it is about.

A 31-page pamphlet by Alexander C. Anderson titled *A Handbook and Map to the Gold Region of Frazer's and Thompson River,* published in San Francisco in 1858, sold for $900; a 12-pager entitled *Articles of an Association by Name of Ohio Co.* published in Worcester in 1789, sold for $1,700. A 1926 pamphlet, *Analyce d'un Entretien,* published in Montreal by Dennis Viger, sold for $50. It isn't only the age that determines the value—old guides or how-to pamphlets are very valuable, as are old advertising pieces from an earlier time. Many mining companies put out pamphlets, and so did individuals—*The New Northwest,* a 24-page pamphlet by Mrs. Linda W. Slaughter, describing the advantages of "Bismarck and Vicinity . . . soil . . . timber . . . climate . . . settlement and etc.," published by Burleigh County Pioneer's Association, is worth $1,200.

When you get into antique collecting you become involved in all phases, whether you intend to or not. A scrap of paper may turn out to be a valuable autograph, a yellowed pamphlet a valuable piece of Americana, and the comic books we read as youngsters may be worth a small fortune. There is so much to learn, so much to look for, since the collectible treasures have many faces and the paper ones are just as valuable as those of metal or glass.

If you wish to collect comic books, you will be interested to know that the Academy of Comic Art Fans and Collectors promotes the development and preservation of this popular art form. It maintains a microfilm library of comics published in one thousand magazines and periodicals. The organization is ten years old and has over two thousand members. It publishes a bi-monthly magazine and sponsors an annual convention. You may write to P. O. Box 7499, North End Station, Detroit, Michigan 48202 for more information.

9.

STAMPS

The first United States postage stamp was issued on July 1, 1847, picturing Benjamin Franklin. Now, a little more than a hundred years later, there are an estimated sixteen million people collecting stamps in the United States alone. Young and old, rich and poor enjoy this fascinating hobby, for it's possible to collect cancelled stamps from your daily mail, to have friends save their stamps for you, and to root through trash, old buildings that are being torn down, and accumulations in attics, all without putting a cent into your hobby.

For a very small investment, the United States Post Office offers you everything you need to become a collector. Among other things they sell "United States Stamps and Stories," illustrating almost all the famous people and historic events from the time of our first stamp to the present day. For another $2, they'll send you a stamp collector's starter kit, containing a 20-page stamp album, stamps with mounting hinges and a pamphlet, *ABC's of Stamp Collecting.*

Collecting stamps is a search that goes on and on. It is important to study the latest stamp catalogs—a good one helps you identify your collected stamps and gives you current values. And it's also a good idea to clip the stamp news from the hobby page of your local

"United States Stamps and Stories," available at United States Post Office for $2. (Photo courtesy U.S. Postal Service)

newspaper and put it into a scrapbook, so you keep informed of what's going on in the stamp world.

Recently I read in the *Washington Post* about an engineering student who was down to his last five dollars when he received word that his "1871 Japanese 500 Mon Dragon Stamp," one of the rarest stamps in the world, had sold at auction in Tokyo for twenty million yen, slightly more than $75,000. Weber had inherited the stamp from his father, who had probably paid 50 cents or $1 for it in 1953.

Stories like this make an amateur (or professional) eager to start looking for that rare or unusual stamp that may bring in a fortune.

But first the amateur must study stamps so that he recognizes an unusual one, if he comes across it.

Here is a list of some of the outstanding United States Philatelic (stamp) publications a serious collector should study:

> *Stamps,* 153 Waverly Place, New York, New York 10014
> *Linn's Stamp News,* Box 29, Sidney, Ohio 45365
> *Scott Monthly Journal,* 10102 F. Street, Omaha, Nebraska 68127
> *Minkus Stamp Journal,* 116 West 32nd Street, New York, New York 10001

Attend every stamp show or auction sale held near you, and see what the stamps are bringing. Often these auctions are held in hotels or motels in large cities. Watch the newspapers for announcements. At important auctions you get a chance to inspect at first-hand the rare specimens that you may never otherwise have a chance to see.

10.

SILVER AND BRASS

When I told a dealer friend that I proposed to include this chapter in my book, she told me it would be impossible for amateurs on a shoestring budget to collect silver. I not only disagreed with her, but set out to prove that she was wrong. This book is not written on theory but on practice, and the bargains I tell you about are still available today.

Silver purchased in one day for $18.60, in 1974. (Photo by Ross Chapple)

To show my friend that there is still much old silver around that doesn't cost a fortune, I set out one morning recently with $20 to invest. I visited five thrift shops and one basement sale and came home with eight pieces for the total sum of $18.60. A William Rogers teapot cost me $2; a platter (without marks) $1; a footed large bowl with lacy cover (marked Poole Silver, EPNS) cost $5; a bread tray (Moreware plate) 50 cents; a condiment set (one bottle missing) cost $2; a heavy sterling bracelet, 10 cents; a beautiful English silver stand (minus two bowls) was $5, and a large round tray (Sheridan silverplate) was $3. I bought all this in one day, and I'm sure I could have done even better with more time.

The condiment set alone should bring in a lot more than I spent all day, even with a bottle missing—and I'm sure I'll find a replacement for it. This little excursion proves that you can't afford to listen to well-meaning friends with negative attitudes about collecting—old silver pieces are available, if you just take the time to look for them.

That same silver, after polishing. (Photo by Ross Chapple)

There are a few tips an amateur should know before setting out. Not all silver will be marked. I have always advised my customers to become better acquainted with their druggist, and with a jeweler or pawnbroker. A druggist will be happy to weigh your silver or gold on his troy weight scales—in fact my own druggist in North Carolina would test metals for me with an acid to ascertain whether my silver was sterling, or if my jewelry was solid gold, plated or gold-filled. Although the marks 900 and 925 are acknowledged markings for silver content, I've discovered many sterling pieces marked from 700 to 900 by testing with acid. Mexican and some South American silver was often marked this way. Remember, too, that a thin piece of sterling (like solid 24- and 18-karat gold) is soft and can be bent in the hand. Plated silver is much heavier, usually with three or four coats of silver over it.

One of the best things you can do is to start handling all the metal pieces you come across—after a while you'll get to know fine silver just by the way it feels.

Once I paid 10 cents for a tarnished old piece out of a pile of kitchen pans. It really looked like an old cookie sheet: flat and plain, except for a slightly fluted edge. Back in my shop I discovered (as I had suspected from rubbing the bottom with my fingers) that I had a beautiful sterling tray. The mark was in the fluted edge. If you rub sterling with your fingers, it will begin to clean immediately and there's a feel about sterling that is indescribable.

Pure silver is too soft for practical use and it has always been the practice to alloy it with copper, the amount of copper being strictly legislated since 1300 A.D. by an act of Edward I. In England, misrepresenting hallmarked silver became punishable by death under George II (Act of 1757) and any fraud with hallmarked silver is still a highly felonious offense in England.

In America it was not always so. Before the late 1800's, silver- and goldsmiths were free to mark their wares just about any way they pleased, and you can still find fraudulent markings today.

The earliest of all hallmarks on silver is the leopard's head. (It is always called a leopard's head, though it actually looks like a lion.)

The early leopard is crowned; after 1795, it is uncrowned, and collectors naturally try to find the crowned leopard. Many people think it's the town-mark of London, but it's actually a royal mark granted out of the Royal Arms. The leopard's head was never used in Scotland or Ireland.

The second mark on English silver was the "maker's mark," required by law as an endorsement that the silver was not substandard. This mark might be a sign or symbol used by the craftsman to distinguish his shop. In later years, many silversmiths used their initials, and in some cases a symbol plus initials. Following these marks was the "date letter," generally in the form of a shield.

A good source for studying English hallmarks is *Silver Collecting for Amateurs* by James Henderson. Hallmarks on English silver are the way to tell where and when a piece was made, and by whom. Much of the old silver we find in America was made in England, and it's good to know your marks.

Here in America metals have a long and fascinating history, for many Colonial farmers had their own workshops and hammered silver and gold into all sorts of things, some marked, some not. Many people had silver coins made into useful articles, since there were no banks then, and a family was noted for its wealth by the number of silver plates and teapots they owned. In those early days, silversmiths traveled like peddlers from village to village, staying long enough to produce household wares from coins. These are referred to as "coin silver" pieces, and if you find them they, too, are likely to be hidden under layers of tarnish.

Silver spoons are among the most popular collectibles today. Many of the early spoons were handmade and often in special designs for specific owners. In Pittsburgh, I came across two large serving spoons of coin silver, one set with two garnets in the handle, dated 1834; the other with three garnets, dated 1835. Obviously they had been made to commemorate an anniversary of some sort.

As early as 1889, M. W. Galt, in Washington, D.C., put out the first known souvenir spoons with the heads of Martha or George Washington on top of the handle. After that, souvenir spoons became a sort of fad in this country, and other silversmiths came out with spoons depicting witches, soldiers and other characters on the handles. Today you'll find all sorts of spoons in various metals commemorating the Apollo flights, Presidents, holidays such as Christmas, Easter and Mother's Day—there are even spoons with cartoon characters on them. A collector has a wide field to select from, old and new, all collectible, and most of them are advertised from time to time in various magazines and newspapers. The *Downs* catalog (sent free on request to Dept. 474, 1014 Davis Street, Evanston, Illinois 60204) lists a wide selection of spoons, all with illustrations.

Frequently, I've had not-so-pretty pieces of sterling in my shop that would bring in more by weight—as scrap—than I could get by selling them. Often, too, as silver and gold are soft and bend easily, many of the old pieces became damaged and are worth more as scrap. All in all, over the years I've made quite a bit of money on my scrap silver and gold. You can do the same—if you have a troy weight scale at your disposal and know the going rate for these metals, you can quickly ascertain what a piece is worth. The exchange rates fluctuate so much these days (usually rising), that it would be impossible to list them accurately here.

I always rummage through bins of silver flatware for sterling pieces. The fact that they may be bent or damaged never deters me from buying. The same is true of damaged candle holders, for you can usually buy them cheaply, and after the weighing materials are removed, the silver weight mounts up. Some of the things to look for that make good scrap are old silver or gold eyeglass frames, compacts, flatware, class rings, mutilated silver toilet sets (brushes and mirrors), backs of military brushes, candlesticks and, of course, jewelry (which I'll discuss in the next chapter).

I always keep a scrap box for these metals, and once or twice a year I send them away (after my druggist weighs them, of course) to a company that buys silver and gold.

Unfortunately, the company I've used for thirty years has gone out of business, but there are many others (including some pawnbrokers and jewelers) who will buy scrap gold and silver. I suggest

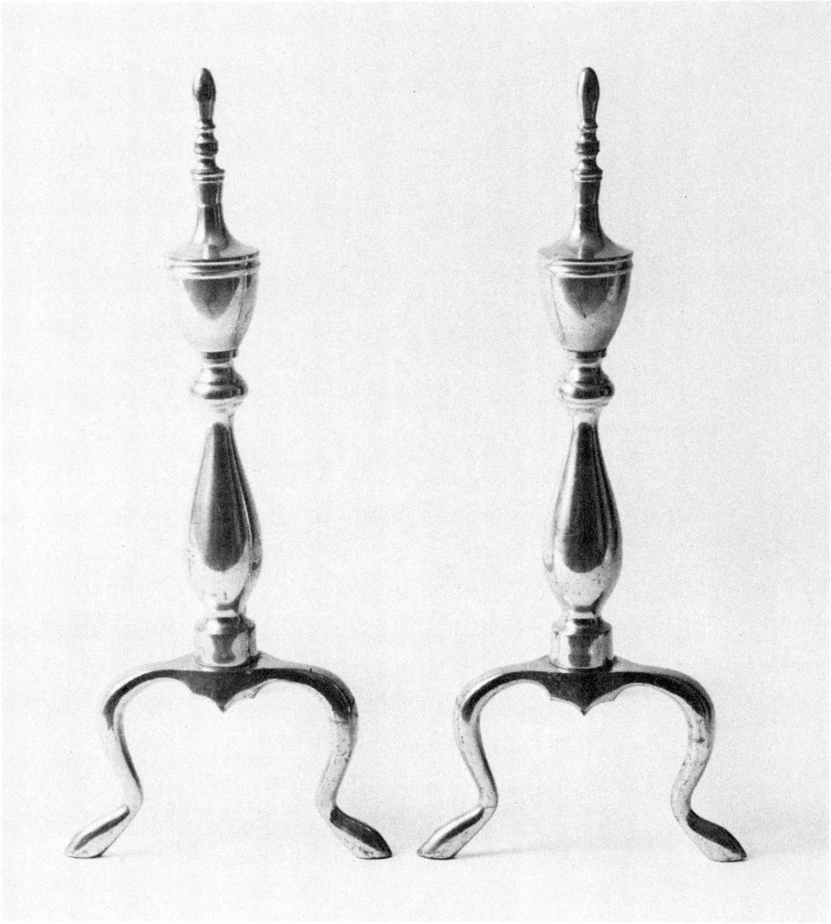

Andirons, purchased tarnished and disassembled for 25 cents, in 1974. (Photo by Ross Chapple)

that you look for them under *Gold, Silver and Platinum Buyers* in the yellow pages of your phone book. If you live in a small town which has no yellow pages, visit the library and look for the yellow pages of a nearby city. If the library doesn't have them, ask your local newspaper to let you see theirs—newspapers usually have phone books from all over the country. It's a good idea to write the company first and ask their rates for silver and gold. And be sure to insure your package when sending it through the mails.

When I go on a buying trip, there are three things I always carry with me: a pocket knife to scratch through paint; a magnifying glass for viewing the smallest hallmarks on silver, gold or china, and a small magnet for testing brass—brass will not attract a magnet. Many times old andirons or pots will look for all the world like iron, when in reality they are brass (worth far more) that has tarnished black. This is where your magnet comes in: if they don't attract it, they're brass—but chances are you can still buy them *as iron,* for many dealers never bother to test them. I once bought brass andirons, tarnished and disassembled, in a basket of junk for 25 cents. Polished and assembled, they were pretty and very salable.

Your magnet will also tell you if something is *not* brass. When I had my shop, people would frequently come to me and say they had a "solid brass bedstead" to sell. Well, most of the hundreds I've bought and sold over the years were not solid brass at all, but brass plate over iron frames. This is where your magnet comes in again. Unless the brass coating is very thick, the iron will attract the magnet and you will know immediately that it is not solid brass.

11.

JEWELRY

Buying a shoe-boxful of scrap jewelry from a thrift shop is more fun than a treasure hunt. When I had my shop in Pittsburgh, five Salvation Army stores used to save all their jewelry for me. It usually came in shoe boxes and cost me $1 or perhaps $2, at most. I've found watch fobs of gold, lockets with chip diamonds in them, gold chains (often matted together), cameo brooches, *real* pearls and scores of other valuable things.

A lot of small thrift stores would rather sell all their jewelry to one person than put it out and have it stolen. Unless they have a lockable showcase, this is less bother to them. When you go into a store that doesn't have a showcase, ask for jewelry—you may be surprised to find it hidden under a counter or in the back room.

Contrary to popular opinion, gold will tarnish too, so if you find a tarnished piece with intricate workmanship and no mark, don't automatically discard it as brass. Since gold is soft, the markings on a ring or necklace may literally be worn off. Always have such pieces tested before you decide they're not gold. I've found many rings that were worn all the way through in back, and some that had obviously been cut where they'd most likely become too tight on a finger. Marks on many watch fobs have also become worn by rubbing against the coarse wool of a man's pants.

Contents of a $2 jewelry box bought in 1974. (Photo by Ross Chapple)

On the other hand, always test the markings you do find. Back in Pittsburgh several years ago, I bought a box of open-faced gold watches for $50. Two of them were marked 18K. and 24K. respectively. I figured their gold content alone would be worth more than the price of my bid, but upon testing the watches later I found that all of them—including those marked—were gold plated. In England, that fraudulent marking would have been a crime.

I made another important discovery in those Pittsburgh years. Since I found so much jewelry there, I used to sell it to dealers for antique shows. Through one of my dealers I met a lapidarist who used to visit me once a week, looking for stones. He showed me many pieces of old brass jewelry actually set with semi-precious stones. Once I had a brooch made of brass that was set with eight garnets. So, if you find a pretty, old piece of brass jewelry whose stones are *not coated* in back yet have the sparkle of very good jewelry, take care—they may not be the cheap imitations you think they are, but real stones. Remember, there were not as many paste imitations in the old days as there are today.

There are times when it pays to try to borrow money on a piece of jewelry you suspect may be exceptionally good—a diamond or ruby, say. If you're able to get a loan from a pawnbroker, you'll soon find out if it is good, for he will usually lend you about a third or a quarter of its retail value. If you ask him outright about a piece and he says it's no good but wants to buy it anyway—*don't sell!* All dealers are not as honest as you'd like them to be.

Anytime I find beads of any kind strung on sterling or gold chains, I suspect right away that they may be good—it's logical to assume that the owner would not have had dime store beads strung on sterling or gold. This is where your friendly jeweler or pawnbroker can be a big help.

For years I found more pearls than anything else in the boxes of jewelry I bought, and I'd sell them for very little. Then I acquired a regular customer from the British Embassy in Washington who came in every Sunday just to buy pearls. I became suspicious after a while, and called the Japanese Embassy to find out how I could tell *real* or *cultured* pearls from paste. They told me to hold the pearls between my teeth, and if they felt gritty they most likely were good. After that I always tested. I found many gritty pearls and took them to a jeweler to be X-rayed. I generally discovered that they were indeed good pearls.

Whenever you buy pearls, watch out for clasps that say "Japan" on them. Most of our pearls come from there and that alone is enough to make you cautious. Here, too, watch out for sterling chains and clasps. Examine the beads, separately, to see if any of them are peeling. The Japanese Embassy assured me that pink pearls are more valuable than white. I was also told that Japanese women would never wear pearls in the kitchen, for heat is very bad for them. However, a jeweler I know says he doesn't believe that heat hurts the real ones.

While amateurs on shoestring budgets are not likely to be out buying expensive antique jewelry, they can have a lot of fun experimenting with trading other antique items (especially ones you get for practically nothing) for solid gold jewelry, regardless of whether it's beautiful or not. Just remember that the higher the karat the purer the gold, and that troy weight (by which gold is measured) has 12 ounces to the pound (not the usual sixteen).

Also remember that broken jewelry is usually a good buy, for the metals are salable and so are the stones, and often you can buy broken pieces for very little. When you don't see broken jewelry in a shop, ask for it and never examine it too closely—take a chance if the price is low, and do your examining at home. Curb your enthusiasm when you find a whole box. Ask for the price on all of it, although you know there is much you will not want. Get dealers to sell you the whole box, for in the long run it will pay off.

12.

DOLLS

From the beginning of time, one of man's oldest habits seems to have been making images of himself. Dolls have been very important in all early civilizations we know of. They have been unearthed in tombs in Egypt and in American Indian burial mounds. In ancient China, fine porcelain and ivory dolls were used by female patients to point out to the doctors where they felt their own pains. In Japan in ancient times, and still today, a doll festival is held when the Sakura trees are in bloom. Primitive people made dolls to represent their enemies and used them in all sorts of ceremonial and voodoo practices. In many tribes the faces of dolls were left blank, for there was a superstition that once the doll face was painted on, it came into possession of a soul. Dolls were thought to hold spirits, either friendly or evil. As civilization progressed, dolls were relegated more and more to children as toys to love and care for. First came the "mama dolls," then the crying dolls, and now we have walking, talking, eating, and wetting dolls.

Dolls, like paintings and literature, have always been representative of their own era and part of its history. Victorian dolls were fatter, for that was fashionable then. Dolls from the flapper era had bobbed hair and were flatchested. Dolls of the nineteen-fifties wore

Dolls, each purchased in 1974 for $2 or less. (Photo by Ross Chapple)

high-heeled shoes, and many dolls of today are black, reflecting the revival of black culture.

Before World War II, there were very few doll collectors, for the collectible dolls were scarce and quite expensive. Collections then were almost entirely composed of bisque dolls from France and Germany, and early English porcelains. Then, during the War, doll collecting underwent a great change.

American soldiers, sailors and marines began sending home costume dolls from the various countries around the world in which they served. Almost every child of an American serviceman could boast a doll or two from Europe, Japan or the Pacific Islands. In many homes, the old china closets were emptied of their dishes and converted into cabinets for collections of dolls, many of which were handmade and dressed in native costumes.

These World War II dolls, which were so inexpensive to buy at that time, have become valuable in the collecting business today. Most were made of hard composition materials (although some were made of cloth), so expertly stuffed and handpainted that they resembled china.

Today, any doll not made of soft plastic is collectible. Since few amateur collectors on shoestring budgets are likely to find the old bisque and porcelain dolls, and could not afford them if they did, they should start their collections with the oldest composition head-and-hand dolls that have stuffed cloth bodies, arms and legs. Most of these forty- or fifty-year-old dolls are frequently found in rummage sales, for they were not always pretty. Few had eyes that opened and closed; more often their faces (and eyes) were painted on, and the years of abuse have usually taken their toll. Frequently the paint has faded or been washed off the faces and the cloth bodies have spilled their insides—but these dolls can be repaired and are worth it.

Of course, some of these composition dolls did have eyes that opened and closed, and hair instead of painted heads, but they are becoming harder and harder to find. Many of the painted-faced dolls were boy dolls, dressed in romper-type clothes.

Kewpie dolls have become very collectible now. When Rose O'Neil began her first drawings of the Kewpie around the turn of the century, she probably had no idea that the adorable cherub-type figure would become one of the most popular dolls in hundreds of collections. Today there are Kewpie clubs all over the country and they hold conventions every year in various cities.

In the early 1900's, Kewpie dolls were inexpensive, frequently made of celluloid, plaster or chalk, and were offered as prizes at state fairs and carnivals, or sold over the counter in almost all five-

and-ten-cent stores. They varied in size, but the faces were always those of baby-innocence, with a painted peak of raised hair on top of an otherwise bald head. A very few Kewpies were made of bisque, and even the small 3-inch bisque dolls bring as much as $50 today. The cheaper variety, which sold for $1 or less originally, bring from $7 to $25 in shops today, and a friend of mine recently paid over $100 for a jointed Kewpie of hard composition.

The amateur collector should never pay more than a few dollars for a Kewpie—in fact, unless you really know what it is worth, you should hesitate to pay more than $5 for any doll. Rummage sales and the toy collections in charity stores are the best places to find them.

Character dolls are the most popular ones to collect today. Shirley Temple dolls from the 1930's and 1940's are in big demand—most of them were made by the Ideal Toy Company and many of them bring as much as $45. (In fact, all Shirley Temple toys and artifacts are collectible—a two-foot paper doll sells for around $12, and a Shirley Temple wicker doll carriage is listed at $100 in many antique books.)

A hard plastic Margaret O'Brien doll is listed at $18; Ideal dolls of Deanna Durbin and Judy Garland (25-inch and 15½-inches) sell for $37 and $30, respectively. A set of Snow White and the Seven Dwarfs, made of painted cloth and put out by Ideal in 1937, is worth up to $250 in their original box. A set of the Dionne quintuplets (each 7 inches) from around 1936 or 1937, with their names embroidered on each doll and on the swing seats is worth $175 in mint condition.

Any doll that represents a person or character will one day be worth a great deal. These are the ones to look for and hold on to. So are the first Tiny Tears (made of hard rubber) and the first Betsy Wetsy.

Handmade cloth (rag) dolls are good, too. At a bazaar recently I saw a *new* handmade Raggedy Ann doll sell for $45. Boudoir dolls and pin-cushion doll heads are also very collectible. Most of these were popular during the twenties and had the "flapper" look. Some were made in Germany; though many were made in Japan.

If you decide to collect dolls, never pass up doll heads or parts of doll bodies, for there are doll hospitals in almost every city where experts can do beautiful restoring jobs. Also you'll frequently be able to trade in doll parts for the cost of your own repair job. One doll doctor tells me that finding old parts is becoming almost impossible, and it's often necessary to buy new parts for repairs.

If you're interested in finding doll clubs in your town, look in the yellow pages of the phone book for "Dolls, Repairing." Repairers will most likely know just about every doll collector in your area.

13.

FURNITURE THAT'S EASY TO FIND AND WORTH BUYING

For several years round-top trunks have been selling for outrageous prices, but the so-called "step-sister" flat-tops have been selling for as little as $1. In 1973 I found two such trunks in an alley near my home awaiting the trash pickup, and I paid a neighbor's son $1 to drag them to my back door. Only one trunk had a tray, but they were both substantially in good condition. Earlier the same year, I had also paid $1 for another such trunk

Curved-top trunk, circa 1900, stripped. (Photo by Ross Chapple)

Flat-top "step-sister" trunk, circa 1900, stripped. (Photo by Ross Chapple)

from Sloan's auction house. The auctioneer couldn't even get another bid on it, so I think I am correct in saying the flat-top trunks can be bought for practically nothing—and they're very desirable, if you know what to do with them.

I made over the two alley trunks for my two daughters. My first task was to hose them off, and then I took them into the basement. There I set about pulling off all the old canvas-like fabric covering. It took six hours to strip the first trunk, and I found the wood underneath to be beautiful old pine, mellowed with age. I sanded it the following day, removing all the remaining spots of glue left from the fabric. The wood required no stain, for its age had produced exactly the shade I wanted. With fine steel wool and varsol, I scrubbed the hardware (hinges, trim and catch) and discovered they were brass.

When the trunk was completely cleaned off, I used a quick-drying, satin finish varnish on the whole thing, including the hardware. Varnish gave the brass a protective covering so that it would not tarnish darker than the desired mellow look I had obtained by scrubbing—an old trunk or other old piece would be spoiled with too-shiny brass fixtures.

The old paper lining came off quite easily by wetting it, and then came the job of repapering. If you want a trunk to look authentic, use an antique-looking wallpaper—one with small flowers or calico pattern is especially good. It is much easier when you use pre-pasted paper—all you have to do is wet the paper and apply it. A friend of mine uses fabrics to line her trunks and they are beautiful, but working with cloth is difficult for me, for smoothing out wrinkles is not an easy task and requires more patience than I have.

The end results, in either case, are lovely trunks that will bring you at least $50 in an antique show. More and more dealers are beginning to realize the potential value of these flat-top trunks, so I would advise you to buy as many as possible, even if you have to store them for future use. They are bound to increase in value as time goes on and they become harder to find. An excellent how-to trunk book may be ordered from *Dorothymae's Trunks, Ltd.,* Box 536, Spearman, Texas 79801.

Old kitchen tables are another item you can buy for very little. Aside from coats and coats of paint, many of them have layer after layer of oilcloth stuck to their tops. They come in varied shapes and sizes—the small ones make beautiful end tables or lamp tables, when refinished. The medium and larger sizes, cut down to make handsome coffee tables and, of course, the larger ones are ideal as dining tables. Most are of pine or oak (although I've found several of walnut), and most of them are handmade.

Recently I bought an old kitchen table at the Salvation Army store for $3. When I pulled out the drawer, I saw that it had been put together with pegs and that the wood was pine. It has fairly large, turned legs with porcelain casters on them. There are six lay-

Walnut handmade dropleaf table (possibly late 19th century), with Victorian castors, bought in Salvation Army Alley store for $4, in 1974.

ers of oilcloth stuck on, and after they were scraped off the top turned out to be three wide pine boards. My husband used lye and hot water to remove the paint. Again, the old wood had so mellowed with age that no stain was needed, and the finished table would bring $100 or more in any antique shop, for these old kitchen tables are beautiful when refinished and will fit in almost any home.

Dresser mirrors are another item that can be bought for a song and restored to beauty and value. Old dressing tables (vanities) of the twenties and thirties had three-fold mirrors which have often been separated from their original bases. In fact, many people used to break the vanity apart, separating the two sides, each of which usually had two or three drawers, to make end tables or bedside tables out of them. The mirrors often go begging at auctions, despite the fact that they are usually framed in walnut or mahogany and are of heavy plate glass. I buy every one I can get for a few dollars—then I take off the two sides and am left with a beautiful full-length mirror that enhances the end of a hall or the top of a stairway. We always take out the glass and refinish the frames, and after my husband fills in the small holes where the hinges were attached, few people would ever suspect that the finished product had once been part of a vanity.

Almost all dresser mirrors also have potential value and beauty, once the frames are refinished. The plate glass is of much higher quality than you find in mirrors today, and they come in all shapes and sizes. The ovals and rounds are especially desirable, so never pass up a dresser mirror that can be bought for a dollar or two.

Buffets or sideboards are other pieces of furniture that can be purchased for very little. Because of their size and weight, many folks shy away from them. The moving cost is generally more than the purchase price, but I seldom pass up a pretty one. Almost all of these pieces were made of very good woods. I bought two Empire ones for $5 each, to use with my round dining table.

Sideboard, purchased for $5 at Sloan's, in 1973.

I also have two others which I use for an entirely different purpose. One of mahogany that I bought for $3 has three center drawers and cabinets on each side. It had very long legs, which we immediately cut off, bringing the cabinet down to within three inches of the floor. On top of it I centered an open-faced mahogany bookcase, and it makes a beautiful breakfront for my studio. The sides are perfect for filing manuscripts, the drawers have a multitude of uses for storing papers and stationery, while the open shelves make it convenient for me to find the books I want. The whole thing cost me less than $10, for we moved both pieces in our station wagon. So any time you have an opportunity to buy one of those dining sets from the twenties, with china cabinet and buffet with long legs, take it, convert the china cabinet and buffet as we did, and you'll have a lovely breakfront, taking up less room and looking far prettier than the originals.

Old beat-up gold leaf frames are another prize to look for. Often, when the plaster of paris is broken and much of it gone, a frame can

Five of six damaged frames purchased for $20 job lot. (Photo by Ross Chapple)

One of six damaged frames from $20 lot, restored with a $2.40 window-glass mirror. (Photo by Ross Chapple)

be bought for very little. We soak ours (in bathtub or vat) until all the plaster comes off. The wood underneath is usually beautiful pine, which refinishes so well that these frames bring fantastic prices at sales. We accumulate them and usually put eight or ten in a show at once and have received as much as $50 apiece for them. If you decide to collect frames, you can always find a ready market with artists, decorators and antique shops when you decide to sell.

Frame of old Singer sewing machine purchased for $2. (Photo by Ross Chapple)

The old treadle sewing machine frames and cabinets can be purchased for very little, and will become more valuable as time goes on. Most early machines were made of golden oak, mounted on an iron frame. The entire machine, with wood refinished and iron painted black, makes a decorative lamp table. If you find one complete with inner works, by all means preserve the whole machine, for (like the first phonographs) one day the machine will become much more valuable as a working piece of Americana than the cabinet alone.

I have one on which I mounted a Duncan Phyfe dropleaf table top taken off a damaged base. Securely mounted to the machine base, the drop leaves operate perfectly and it makes an ideal dining table for a small apartment where space is at a premium. I use mine as a side table for a silver coffee service, but often it is pulled out and opened for card playing. Many antique shops sell the iron bottoms with marble tops—the weight of the marble is sufficient to hold it without any attachment. There are so many ways one can use these bases. A friend has placed a climbing plant on the treadle and allowed it to climb around the ornate frame of her machine, making it a conversation piece.

Dropleaf table top from damaged Duncan Phyfe table (cost $3), mounted on sewing machine base. (Photo by Ross Chapple)

Odd, single kitchen chairs can often be bought for $1 or $2, for there are many people who think that chairs should match and come in sets. Far more interesting, I think, is a set of eight *different* chairs. One of my customers was an army major who had traveled around the world. He collected odd dining chairs, and when I met him he had fifteen very pretty odd ones. I added five more to his collection. He said he never had a boring dinner party, for the guests were always so fascinated by his chairs and where he had acquired them that much of the conversation centered around them. A pretty (often crudely made) old kitchen chair makes a lovely side or desk chair when refinished. I buy every one I can find for a dollar or two.

Wooden boxes of almost any variety are good items to buy. Old crates, which used to carry fruits and vegetables to market, were often dove-tailed pine boxes that can be refinished to make pretty boxes to hold magazines or wood or logs beside the fireplace.

Always notice how the boxes are made. Some cheese boxes and older cigar boxes are lovely for sewing notions. I wouldn't bother with a box that is nailed unless it had a hinged top. If such a box is made of heavy wood, the nails could be counter-sunk and the tops of the holes filled in with putty or plastic wood. Many of them can be used effectively for plants.

The drawers from old furniture have many possibilities. Old furniture was made of good woods, and an odd drawer (frequently found in the trash or some rummage house) may make a lovely shadow-box, letter tray or file box. One of the three drawers from the sewing machine base I used for my dropleaf table is now being used as a file box. A 3 by 5 card fits into it perfectly, and the drawer front is ornate and pretty on my kitchen counter. The other two drawers I use for flower boxes for my kitchen window.

There are many other things that can be done with odd drawers. Before you pass them up, think about purposes they might serve, for many times you will get them free since they have little sale value anywhere. Then use your imagination and put them to use.

Sewing machine drawer, just the right size for a file box. (Photo by Ross Chapple)

The most treasured pieces my husband and I look for constantly are the old kitchen cabinets that used to be built-in. They often show up at auction houses. Sometimes they're painted or don't have backs, since they were built to stand against the wall. We have paid as little as $3 for these big cabinets, which we call hutches today, and have sold them, restored, for as much as $500. Almost all of them were made of thick pine. They were always enclosed, either with paneled wooden doors or with glass. They are bulky and difficult to move, but worth the trouble.

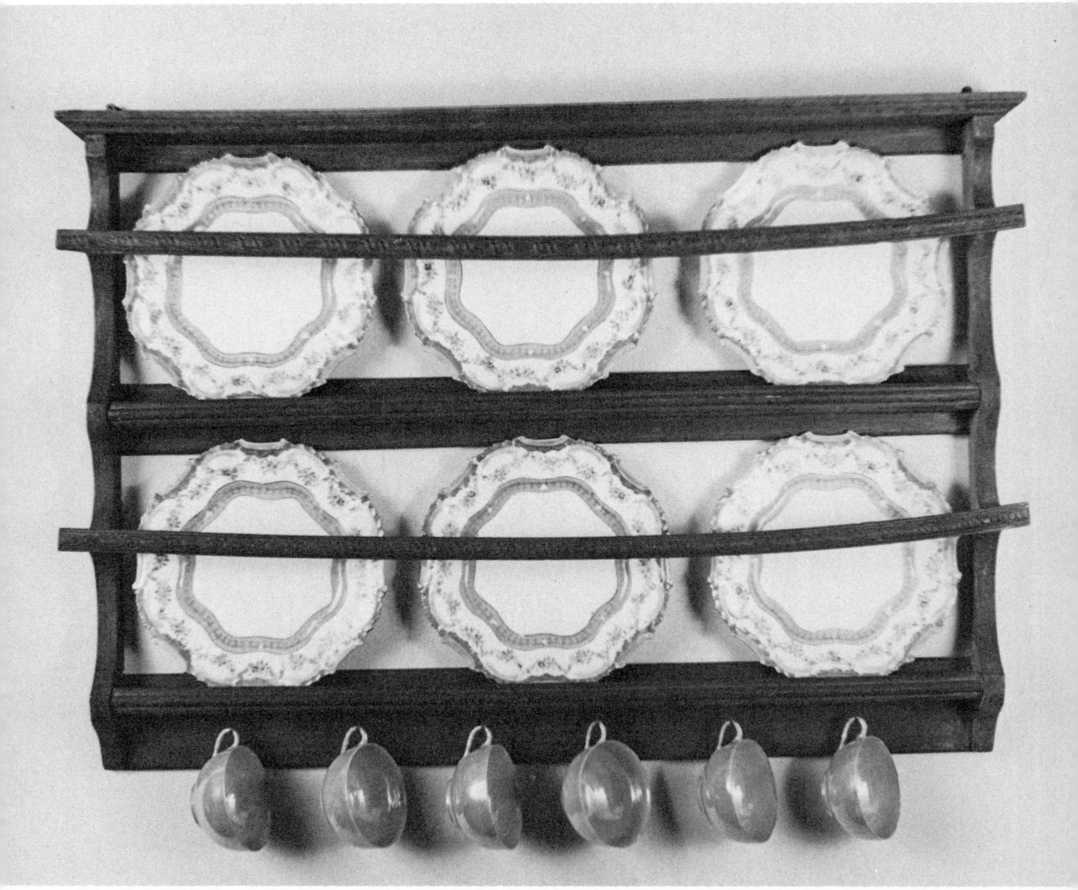

Plate rack made of molding bought at rummage sale, for $3.

Occasionally they're too tall for the average ceilings in homes today, but we frequently cut them down. The place to cut is across the middle, where the tops are attached to the bases—there is usually a two- or three-foot space here, between the top and the base cabinet which provides the working surface. We love the ones with wooden doors, for they are the prettiest when refinished.

Before we moved to Washington, we had three such hutches. They looked so impressive that an auditor from the Sales Tax Division thought we must have made a great deal more money than we claimed, if we could afford such fine furniture. It took some convincing to prove that we didn't have a single hutch that had cost us over $40. My husband's work is superb, and he loves working with old pine and walnut. We rescued one old hutch that had been so badly burned that I didn't think it was worth moving, but it was thick cherry and walnut, I remember, and there wasn't a nail in it. My husband worked for weeks, sanding and scraping, and as a result it turned out to be one of the prettiest cabinets we ever owned.

Wardrobes and old clothes presses are usually available for very little. Since most homes now have adequate closet space, the old wardrobes have been discarded, and they are so big and heavy that few people will bother with them. They, too, can be turned into beautiful, functional pieces. I've seen some dealers buy them and break them up on the spot, removing the larger panels of wood to use in other pieces of furniture. We never broke them up, but bought every one we could get for $10 or $15, if they were of good woods.

My husband collects old table boards (leaves) to use for just such purposes. He often puts them in as shelves from top to bottom, and we sell those wardrobes for linen cupboards or other storage uses. They are useful in small apartments, where you can spare the wall space, for they can hold so many things, while making an attractive addition to any place furnished with antiques. They can be used as room dividers, too.

There are many other pieces that can be bought for very little, despite today's inflationary prices. It just takes a little imagination and a love for the antique "step-children" that few people seem to want. The day will come when all these things will be cherished by collectors—so now is the time to buy, when the prices are low and they are easy to find. You can't possibly lose on any of these things, nor on many, many more which you will learn to recognize as time goes on.

14.

OLD CLOTHES THRIFT SHOPS—HIDDEN SOURCES OF TREASURE

One morning in a thrift shop for used clothing I saw two antique seekers walk in and express great disappointment to discover they'd driven such a long way and found only old clothes. I couldn't suppress a smile, for that very day I'd found a beautiful antique gold brooch on an old dress and had bought the whole thing for 25 cents. Old clothes bins are often a treasure house of finds.

In old clothes thrift shops you find many valuable things besides wearing apparel. A friend once paid a dime for a hand-sewn thirteen-star flag she found in a bin of rags—she sold that flag to a dealer for $50. A few years ago, the same kind of flag was offered for sale at a public auction in a small town in Maryland. Since no one seemed to want it, a young farmer offered $25 for it, "just to take it off the auctioneer's hands." His 13″ x 78″ flag was of linen, with thirteen five-pointed white stars on a field of blue, and seven red and six white stripes—the style of the second official United States flag, the first to be known as the "Stars and Stripes." The design dates back to 1777, and was used by our Navy until 1916. When the owner took his flag for analysis to the Smithsonian Institution's Museum of History and Technology, they told him it had probably been made sometime between 1820 and 1850. It might even have been made as late as 1876—but regardless of the exact date, it was valued at $5,000.

Frequently, when very old people dye their clothing (usually the accumulation of a lifetime, for earlier generations did not discard as we moderns do) is packed up and sent to some charitable organization to be sold in their thrift shop. Because the styles are long out of date, they usually end up in bales of rags to be sold by the pound —but you'll often find some of the finer pieces put up for sale in bins or on racks or tables. I get excited when I smell mothballs in piles of clothing, for to me it indicates that they belonged to an earlier age and have perhaps been stored away for a long time. In such a bin in a church thrift shop not long ago I found two beautiful embroidered Irish linen bedspreads and four monogrammed linen sheets. I paid

Part of a $5 batch of Irish linens, bought from an old clothes bin in a thrift shop. (Photo by Ross Chapple)

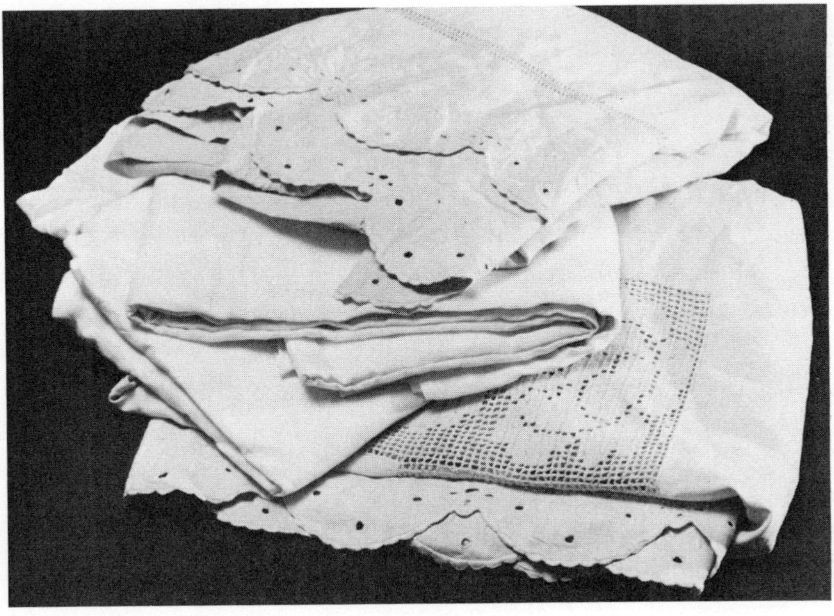

$5 for the lot and could easily get $100 for them. They are all in perfect condition and the spreads have inserts of handmade lace and handcrocheted borders.

Aside from rare linens and pieces of jewelry one may find attached to clothing, there's always the possibility of finding watch fobs in men's pants, old coins in watch pockets and in hidden pockets of men's old suits. You may also find many valuable old buttons, worth a great deal to collectors.

When I had my own shop, I frequented these thrift shops, for my doll collectors would buy old materials, laces and trimmings for doll clothes. I also had several antique-car collectors who were always in the market for clothes from the past to wear in antique-car parades. Theatrical companies, too, were always in the market for period clothes.

Old laces are much sought after today. In 1973 a junk dealer called a young designer in London who was a friend of his and asked if she would like to buy a ton-and-a-half of fabric that was stored in a warehouse. He was willing to sell the lot for 100 pounds, English currency, and the designer grabbed it for her Portobello Road Shop. The price she paid was equivalent to $250 of our currency.

That material turned out to be more than nine thousand different designs and patterns of old lace—probably representing the entire sample range of one mill from 1900 to 1935. They were all colors and materials, with styles ranging from Art Nouveau of the early 1900's to Art Deco of the twenties and thirties, and looking as if they'd been made for curtains and wall hangings.

Those old-but-new designs have since made dresses for an Empress, for the wife of the Governor of one of our Southern states, as well as for movie stars, and her lucky haul made this designer a fantastic reputation as a "dealer in old lace." All kinds of people and museums come to her now, as an authority.

Few of you amateurs have the space to absorb such a large stock, if you were offered it—but the story shows just how valuable old laces can be. The moral is: never pass up any old laces you find in the thrift shop bins. They may be worth a great deal.

Here's one thing to remember when you do find old linens and laces or something of value in the old clothes bins: don't start telling the clerks what you expect to do with them. Act like any normal customer buying old clothes to wear. If you appear eager you will pay more, for clothes are seldom priced in advance—the clerks charge what they think the garments are worth to you. And never go to these shops dressed in your Sunday best or the clerks may soak you with higher prices—they seem to resent well-to-do-looking people who look as if they're slumming. When clerks ask me what I do with all the old things I buy, I simply tell them that I use them for making up quilts, doll clothes and things like that.

No matter what you're collecting, never snub the old clothes bins, for if you find any of the above-mentioned items, you can trade them to a dealer for something else that you really want.

15.

MISCELLANEOUS COLLECTIBLES

No matter what item you think of, somewhere in this country there have got to be people collecting it—and they likely have clubs and papers and annual meetings where they get together and swap and talk about their collections. I can't begin to enumerate all the collectibles here, but I'll just list a few of the most popular. Remember, these are just skimming off the top—the main thing I'd like to show is that if something interests you, go ahead and start collecting it. It's bound to become more valuable with time.

AUTOGRAPHS: Among the many fields of autograph collecting there is none more interesting to American collectors than the Civil War. This, the last "romantic" war for our nation, boasted more leaders, more remarkable individuals than any other in our history. The most sought-after autographs are those of Abraham Lincoln and Robert E. Lee. It is almost impossible to find a document signed by Lincoln for less than $500, though it's possible to find Army vouchers signed by Lee while he was still a lieutenant which sell for around $100.

Confederate autographs are harder to find and more expensive than Yankee ones. There was so much destruction in the South that it is a wonder that any historical documents were preserved, and the quality of Southern paper was poor and not durable. Thus a Stonewall Jackson autograph is worth at least ten times the price of a Ulysses S. Grant. It is almost impossible to find autographs of Generals Jeb Stuart, A. P. Hill or Albert Sidney Johnston, who were killed in the war. Jefferson Davis's autograph is plentiful and can be bought for about $100, but those signed while he was President of the Confederacy are much more expensive. Here the collector must be very careful, for many of Davis's post-war letters were signed by his wife, Varina, who copied her husband's handwriting with considerable skill.

The amateur should be constantly aware that autographs of many persons living today will become collector's items for the future, and preserve them with that in mind.

MILITARY BUTTONS, MEDALS AND OTHER PARAPHERNALIA: Military uniforms have become very popular with our young people as everyday apparel, but I doubt if many ever think to remove the buttons when they discard the jackets and coats. Those buttons are valuable to button collectors as well as collectors of military items—and there are many other military items (regimental patches, flags and equipment) that are fascinating to collect. Anyone interested in collecting military items should send for the *Military Collectors' News,* which is published monthly. The address is P. O. Box 7582Q, Tulsa, Oklahoma 74105. It will help you identify your items, and it has a section, "The Trading Bunker," where you may advertise to trade, buy or sell many of the military items you find.

KNIFE COLLECTING: No matter how sophisticated their surroundings, men have always had use for pocket knives. Today there are almost as many collectors of pocket knives as of guns. Early knives, with their wood, bone and metal handles, are becoming harder to find and quite expensive. Knives from 1760 through 1835 were handmade, often initialed, for most men made their own, marking them with their own styles and hallmarks. Some of the earlier knives, before 1835, had forks attached to the opposite end, for they served many purposes in the lives of the early settlers. After 1835, knives were more or less mass-produced and, of course, these are more plentiful.

A group of knife collectors met recently in the barber shop of Gordon A. Abbott in Dallas, Texas. Mr. Abbott is an avid collector, although he started only a few years ago. He says that there are possibly three hundred pocket knife collectors in Dallas alone, and many with collections worth $7,000 and $5,000. Abbott himself has about two hundred knives in his collection. He says it will soon be hard to find new pocket knives with horn, stag or bone handles. Pearl handles are also being phased out. There are perhaps fifty different brand names of "old knives," which means knives not manufactured any more. If you find an "old knife" that is rare and in mint condition, it could be worth as much as $500.

Remington and Winchester discontinued making knives in the 1930's, although they still manufacture guns. If you find a knife fitted into a case or box, you may have a rare piece. Mr. Abbott's most valuable knife is a Case "Bulldog," a singleblade knife that folds into its handle and comes fitted in a walnut box. In mint condition, he says it is worth $75.

FANS: Most of the fans we collect were imported from Europe or the Far East, but back in 1866, Edward Hunt (who invented the breeches buoy used in life saving by the Coast Guard and the United States Navy) opened the first American fan factory in Weymouth Landing, Massachusetts. He did not receive his patent on the fans until 1868, however. They were made of dark linen and wooden sticks (hornbeam), which took a high polish and did not easily warp. Many were decorated with patriotic scenes prevalent during the Civil War. In 1885 the factory moved and branched out into a variety of designs of painted birds, animals and people. They also put out commercial advertisement fans, and began exporting them to Europe.

Fans come in many varieties: silks, paper, feathers and ivory as well as wood. All fans are collectible and, strangely, some fans made for advertising are as valuable as the fancy ones.

COMBS: Before the flapper era that followed the first World War, it was unheard of for a woman to have bobbed hair. To manage their long tresses, women employed fancy and plain combs. The comb business was quite lucrative and it is obvious that some of the early settlers brought the comb-making know-how to America with them, for as early as 1759, Christopher Anger was advertising his combs in Philadelphia. Combs usually came in three styles—back combs, puff combs and side combs—and, of course, men had folding combs which they could carry in their pockets. They were made of horn, ivory and tortoiseshell, and occasionally of wood and metal. Many of the ladies' fancy back combs were set with jewels, and these are the most sought after by collectors.

BOXES, SMALL AND DECORATED: The fancy velvet and satin Victorian jewelry boxes are perhaps the most popular ones to collect. Just recently I found a beautiful purple velvet box with velvet lining and tray, and with the top elaborately decorated with lacy brass corners and center. I paid $1.75 for it in a thrift shop—it would sell for at least $25 in almost any antique shop.

Old boxes that held silverware are very good, too. I found one recently for 50 cents, made of walnut and lined with velvet. Around the turn of the century, fancy boxes were made for just about every-

Victorian velvet box, brass trimmed, purchased for $1.75 at a thrift shop, in 1974. (Photo by Ross Chapple)

thing. Many were velvet-covered, and a lot were made of silver, brass and woods, trimmed with metals or decorated with paintings. A collector would be safe in paying up to $10 for any pretty Victorian box in good condition. I haven't seen one in an antique show for less than $25 in a long time.

BASEBALL CARDS: Millions of young boys collect baseball cards, and some parents are inclined to look lightly on their enthusiasm. However, thirty million baseball cards were sold last year, and not all to youngsters—collecting them has become both popular and profitable for many elders. Before appraising it as just a harmless hobby, there are a few facts to take into account.

Some cards that sold for a penny in 1950 are now worth $1.50 each. A Homus Wagner baseball card distributed in 1919 on Sweet Caporal cigarettes is worth $1,500 now. This is because Homus Wagner so disapproved of smoking that he withdrew his name, and consequently only a few cards were printed.

An interesting book, *The Great American Baseball Card* by Brendan C. Boyd and Fred Harris is a good source of information on all phases of baseball card collecting.

KITCHEN UTENSILS: All kinds of kitchen utensils—pots, pans and crocks, wooden bowls, spoons, forks and chopping boards—are very worth collecting. Anything made of cast iron sells well—old skillets, waffle irons and cornstick pans, kettles, washpots and dutch ovens. Old enamel ware is good, too. Some of the old coffee pots, kettles, pitchers and pans of gray or blue enamel were pretty and bring high prices at auctions and antique shows. The fact that they may have a few chips should not deter you from buying them. Few pieces found today are in perfect condition, for most of these wares were used daily in the homes of the past.

In fact, almost any old kitchen items, such as tin boxes for matches, salt boxes, toasters from the twenties and thirties that fitted on top of the stove, as well as utensils used in the fireplace or with wood cook stoves, are not only collectible but may be found in almost any rummage sale or thrift shop. An old wooden spoon, which you can often buy for 5 or 10 cents, is worth $1 on the antique market. I have frequently received $3 for a spoon and fork set that cost me a dime.

ROLLING PINS: They made such a variety of these old implements for rolling dough that collecting them can be a fascinating hobby. Most rolling pins made up to and during the 18th century were made by some member of the family as a gift for mother or sister or Aunt Bessie. Most were made of wood—maple, poplar and pine—although many were made of glass, pottery or metal. So long as a rolling pin could be made smooth and round, it didn't much matter what it was made of.

Later on, in the 19th and 20th centuries, fine china and porcelain companies began making rolling pins too—the most popular were Meissen and Delft. As late as 1916, "solid maple rolling pins, 18 inches long, weighing one and one half pounds" were advertised in mail-order catalogs for 8 cents.

Whether it's superstition or not, I can't say, but my mother taught me never to put a wooden rolling pin in water. After making biscuits, she would roll the dough that stuck to the rolling pin with her hands until it all rolled off. Then she'd wipe it with a dry cloth, explaining that if you put water on the pin, your biscuits would not rise or be as light as they should be. I think the real point is that rolling pins were not finished with varnish then as woods are today, and the raw, unfinished wood would absorb the water. A pine or soft wood rolling pin left soaking in water would probably swell out of shape.

Again I would like to emphasize that a single item will not attract a buyer or command as high a price as will a collection. If you accumulate a large assortment of kitchen wares, you may find it easy to sell the entire collection to a dealer, for these are popular items in antique shows. They are small and easily portable, and many dealers travel hundreds of miles to participate in a show.

TINS: Cookie, candy and tea tins, found in many stores today, are very collectible. Many look like the old tea caddies and most are made in England or Holland. These tins are beautifully decorated and are functional besides. I find many of them in thrift shops and at rummage sales, and have never paid over 50 cents for them. My daughter bought four in Europe during the summer of 1973 for 10 cents each. They are very old and the prettiest ones I kept for my collection.

Many tins are of historical interest, too. I have one showing Queen Elizabeth I and Prince Philip on it when they were very young, and another showing Mount Vernon. These tins cost me 10 cents each, and I have refused $5 for them.

Old commercial tins are very collectible and often high-priced. One of the best-selling items during the late 1800's was tobacco packaged in tin lunch pails. The George Washington Plug Tobacco lunch pails, made around 1910, bring about $15 to $40 today.

Mammy's Favorite Brand Coffee came in handy tall pails. Today these pails bring from $18 to $30, depending on condition. Tin store

Old commercial tins found in thrift shops—not one of them cost over 50 cents. (Photo by Ross Chapple)

bins with hinged lids, in which rice, beans, and loose commodities were kept, are also becoming scarce and cost you from $45 up, when you can find them.

Log Cabin syrup tins have always been popular with collectors. Shaped like log cabins, these tins varied slightly over the years from 1888 to 1954, when they were discontinued. A collector can safely pay $3 to $5 for a tin in good condition, for I recently saw one bring

Mammy's Favorite Brand Coffee came in a handy tall pail. Today this type of tin ranges from $18 to $30. Hinged lid store bins, among the most difficult to find, cost $45 and up. (Photo by Ross Chapple)

Log Cabin tin, discontinued in 1954, worth $12 to $15. (Photo courtesy General Foods)

in $12 at a country auction. Within the last five years I have found them in country shops for as little as $1.

Many of the old tin cigarette boxes have kept love letters and important receipts in good condition for many years. Almost all the old tins were converted into useful containers in the home, which is why so many are still on hand. The newer tins I am collecting now will one day join their ranks and become the valuable collectibles from our own time.

COCA-COLA ITEMS: In 1973, the Coca-Cola Company offered copies of their 1912, 1914 and 1916 tin trays for sale for $1.75 each, or the set of three for $4.25. These trays have portraits of pretty, old-fashioned "Coke girls," and are definitely the collectible trays of tomorrow. The original trays are now selling for as much as $25 each. Almost any old Coke item is worth a small fortune. The Coke tray from 1934, showing Johnny Weissmuller and Maureen O'Sullivan, is listed in several antique books at $25. The original Coke 1900 to 1915 "Tiffany type" hanging lamp shade sells for around $500. Old advertisements, bottles, posters and such things are also worth a great deal.

A friend of mine, Bill Ricketts (P. O. Box 9605, Asheville, North Carolina 28805), is considered one of the top Coca-Cola experts in the country. He has thousands of Coke items in his collection and is

Reproduction Coca Cola tray, sold in many shops in 1974 for $1.
(Photo by Ross Chapple)

eager to buy more. Many of his rare items are in the Coca-Cola Company Museum. He pays fair prices and welcomes any correspondence from anyone with things to sell. He would enjoy hearing from people interested in this field of collecting. He will also buy items of other soft drink brands such as Dr. Pepper, Pepsi-Cola, Hires Root Beer and others. Collectors in these fields often contact him when they have old Coke items they wish to trade for their own collections.

Bill Ricketts, the "Cola King," with a small part of his collection. (Photo courtesy Bill Ricketts)

All the Coke bottles from 1894 to 1970. (Photo courtesy Bill Ricketts)

The quest for Coke collectibles is almost endless. To name a few: change receivers, change trays, serving trays, syrup dispensers, lamp shades, pocket mirrors, watch fobs, book marks, thermometers, periodical advertisements, bottle openers, pencil sharpeners, trade tokens, miniature bottles, amber bottles, display bottles, coasters, ash trays, money clips, seltzer bottles, paperweights, snack bowls, glasses, mugs, book covers, key chains, thimbles, playing cards, note pads, calendars, posters, matches, clocks, music boxes, advertising signs, menus, sheet music, blotters, rulers, ice picks, games such as checkers and dominos, needle cases, cooler boxes—the list goes on and on. . . .

Reproduction of the original early 1900's Pepsi tray with six old-time Pepsi fountain glasses, offered via mail only for $2.98 in 1973. (Photo by Ross Chapple)

CHILDREN'S TOYS: Around Christmas time each year the Salvation Army stores and other charitable thrift stores put out the toys accumulated during the year. Even though you are not interested in toys as such, rummage through them. Buy any cheap toy made of cast iron, heavy metal or tin. A riding car I bought for $1 two years ago is listed at $35 in an antique book. If you have storage space and visit thrift shops and sales often, buy any of the above-mentioned toys and hold on to them. With each year they will increase in value, unlike the new toys which are being made of plastic and will never survive to become antiques from this era.

All toy furniture is collectible. Any old wooden or iron doll bed is much in demand. Many of the wooden ones were handmade. Not long ago I stopped to price a tiny doll trunk in an antique store window and was shocked to learn it was priced at $100. Anything in miniature is desirable today and brings a high price. Many collectors do not have room to collect full-sized things and become avid collectors of "mini" furniture, toys, dolls and other tiny things.

Doll bed, circa 1920, found in thrift shop for $5 in 1974. (Photo by Ross Chapple)

You'll find many items worth collecting advertised in newspapers and magazines. If you see an advertisement for a special sale of any modern copy of something old, buy it. A few years ago one of the major insurance companies gave their clients beautiful sets of reproductions of Currier and Ives prints. Many of them reappeared in antique shops for as much as $10 each. Frequently magazines and newspapers will advertise copies of old file boxes originally put out by butter companies, baking powder can banks; old Sears & Roebuck catalogs, and various other things. By all means send for them when you can, for many are exact copies of the originals, and are not marked "reproduction."

There is no way I can list all the collectibles of tomorrow. This list, however, should give you an idea of what to look for and what types of things to save. Celluloid items are collectible, but most plastics are not. Learn to distinguish the difference. Iron, metal, wood and glass are collectible materials; laminated woods and nonreturnable bottles are not. It doesn't take long to learn the difference between materials on sight. Always bear in mind that to be collectible, an item must be able to stand the test of time—it must be durable to become an authentic antique at some time in the future.

CENTENNIAL AND BICENTENNIAL MEMENTOES: I'd like to end with our own Centennial mementoes, past and present. Even amateurs know instinctively that mementoes from the 1876 Centennial are extremely collectible and very valuable. What I want to impress on my readers is the importance of collecting all the mementoes from our Bicentennial, 1976. Within a few years almost every souvenir, program, newspaper and advertisement relating to the Bicentennial will become valuable, as pieces of Americana. I suggest you use scrapbooks (the kind that don't need glue) to house your collection. What an opportunity it is for young people to preserve valuable material for their children. The Bicentennial offers so many mementoes—stamps, coins, programs, newsprint, plates and figurines, and endless other souvenir items—and they are not only part of our history, but also bound to be the valued collectibles of tomorrow.

"The Little Seamstress," calendar from the late 1800's, bought for $3 and framed for 50 cents. (Photo by Ross Chapple)

16.

HOW TO GET FREE APPRAISALS

A very wealthy man I know has a medical check-up every year and it doesn't cost him a dime. It seemed a little preposterous to me at first, for he can well afford the best medical care in our city. However, he feels that paying for a routine check-up is a waste of money, when, as he says, "you can get the best check-up in town for free." What he does is simply to apply for a large insurance policy—if it's for ten thousand dollars or more, you can be sure the company looks him over very carefully. Sometimes he takes out the insurance, but most of the time he doesn't—he just says he'll think about it and let them know.

Now that I think about it, I can see that his method is somewhat similar to the one I use in getting free appraisals on antiques. Here's how you can go about it too.

If your city has a well-established auction house whose reputation is respected in the community, you will find the auctioneers very useful in determining the value of almost any antique. If the piece is small, take it in (not on auction day), and ask the auctioneer or appraiser to estimate how much your piece could get at auction. Then listen to him.

If your piece is very valuable, he may suggest that you place it in the next catalog sale. Most auction houses have one or two of these a year. Owners of property listed for auction may set the minimum price they will take, and the bidding must start at that point.

If you have something too large to transport, you may call the auctioneer and ask him to come to your home (at his convenience) to give you his estimate. Of course, you must give him the impression that you want him to sell it and are not simply seeking a free appraisal.

There are other ways available to you. In most newspaper classified ads, you will find a section under the heading "Items WANTED." If an antique shop is asking for antiques, call them and tell them you have a piece of furniture that you would like to sell, and describe it to the best of your ability. If you think it's old but don't know how old, or what exactly it is, tell them so. Strangely, an antique dealer will respond quicker than an auctioneer to people who don't know what they have. A dealer always hopes it will turn out to be something rare and valuable that he may buy for very little. When the dealer comes to see your piece, listen to everything he says about it. If he wants to buy it, you may assume it actually is antique. If the offer is substantial you may assume that it is valuable, for the dealer must make a profit in reselling. If you're attentive, you may find out what you want to know about your piece, for antique dealers, on the whole, are very generous in sharing their knowledge.

If you have furniture, there is yet another way to get free appraisals. Call a reputable furniture refinisher and ask him to come and give you an estimate on refinishing the piece. While he is there, ask questions about it. A good refinisher knows his furniture. I must emphasize the word *good,* for there are amateurs who open little refinishing shops, but who know so little about good woods that they literally murder a valuable piece. My husband has had many experiences in trying to redeem antiques that had been ruined by belt sanders and thick varnishes. As I always say, call on reputable people, whether you are selling, buying or getting appraisals.

Oil paintings and old prints also need expert appraisal, for very valuable pictures have been sold for a fraction of their worth because the seller didn't know what he had. Once I bought a huge old oil painting at auction. It must have been at least six feet tall, and the colors were so dark you could hardly see the figure of a man standing beside a chair. The auctioneer kept begging for a bid and nobody could have been more shocked than I when I heard myself call out, "One dollar," and had the painting knocked down to me. I hadn't the slightest idea what I'd do with it. It couldn't possibly hang in my shop, which had only an eight foot ceiling. Then I remembered Sloan's, and that an entirely different crowd attended their auctions. I brought that painting to Sloan's for resale, and it brought $57 at their next acution. I never found out what the painting was or who bought it, but there is a nagging thought that it may have been much more valuable than I realized.

Museums are the best places for appraisals of paintings. Every large city has one and the curators are usually very friendly. Again I urge you to seek the experts, for few antique dealers know the true value of art pieces. In fact, small antique shops are the best places to find valuable paintings for reasonable prices. Many artists used symbols (like Whistler's tiny butterfly), and did not always sign their names. It is always exciting to come across a painting with an odd marking—why would an unknown artist or student go to the trouble to hide his identity?

If you have old coins and medals that you do not find listed in current catalogs take them *personally* to the shops that specialize in them. Never mail them in, for seeing the dealer's face and being able to ask him questions may mean many dollars to you. It is possible to come across a rare coin or medal not listed in your catalog. You may find one of a kind or a mistake made in minting, like that penny on the dime proof planchet. If you find such a coin, it is wise not to take the first offer. Get offers from several dealers and compare them before you sell.

If you find an old flag, Mrs. Grace Cooper, Curator of the Division of Textiles of the Smithsonian Institution's Museum of History and Technology, is qualified to appraise it. Signatures and autographs may be sent (by registered mail) to Dr. Percy Powell, Library of Congress Division of Manuscripts, for appraisal.

As for jewelry, I have already stressed the importance of becoming acquainted with a jeweler or pawnbroker in your area. They are your best sources for free appraisals of gold, silver and jewelry. A pawnbroker must be expert in his field, otherwise he would lose a fortune lending money on fakes. A Pittsburgh pawnbroker taught me more about silver, gold and jewelry than I could ever have learned from books.

In buying, selling, trading or getting appraisals on antiques, a lot of psychology comes into play. You must learn when to play dumb, and when to hide your ignorance, for there are times when either of these may put many dollars in your pocket. It's something you can only learn by doing—but, to me at least, it makes collecting the most fascinating business in the whole world.

Good luck and good hunting. I hope this book will add a little excitement and inspiration to every amateur on a shoestring budget who decides to join me in collecting.

Antiques Publications

Hobbies
(The magazine for collectors)
Published by Lightner Publishing Corporation
1006 South Michigan Avenue
Chicago, Illinois 60605

Spinning Wheel
(The national magazine about antiques)
Fame Avenue
Hanover, Pennsylvania 17331

The Antiques Journal
P. O. Box 88128
Dunwoody, Georgia 30338

The Antique Trader
P. O. Box 1050
Dubuque, Iowa 52001

Coin World
P. O. Box 150
119 East Court Street
Sidney, Ohio 45365

Collector's World
Drawer L
Conroe, Texas 77301

Collector's World Bottles and Relics
Route 8, Box 369-A
Austin, Texas 78703

Gems and Minerals
P. O. Box 687
Mentone, California 92359

Military Collectors News
P. O. Box 7582
Tulsa, Oklahoma 74105

Numismatic Scrapbook Magazine
P. O. Box 150
Sidney, Ohio 45365

The Old Bottle Magazine
Box 243
Bend, Oregon 97701

Scott's Monthly Journal
(Stamp collectors)
10102 F. Street
Omaha, Nebraska 68127

Western Collector
511 Harrison Street
San Francisco, California 94105

Flea Market Quarterly Almanac
P. O. Box 243
Bend, Oregon 97701

Collectors' Clubs

Universal Autograph Collector's Club (International)
1211 Avenue I
Brooklyn, New York 11230
Publication: *The Pen and Quill* (monthly)

Auto License Plate Collector's Association
P. O. Box 1017
Chandler, Arizona 85224
Publication: Newsletter (bi-monthly)

Mechanical Bank Collector's Club of America
c/o Albert Davidson
905 Manor Lane
Bayshore, New York 11706
Publication: *Mechanical Bank Collector's Journal* (3 times a year)

Playing Card Collector's Association
Route 3, Box 603
Venetian Village
Lake Villa, Illinois 60046

American Political Item Collectors
4144 S. E. Clinton Street
Portland, Oregon 97202

International Post Card Collectors Association
6380 Wilshire Blvd., Suite 907
Los Angeles, California 90048

The Spooner (spoon collectors)
Route 1, Box 49
Shullsburg, Wisconsin 53586
Publication: *The Spooner* (monthly)

Musical Box Society International
1765 E. Sudan Circle
Greenville, Mississippi 38701
Publication: *Music Box Society Bulletin* (5 per year)

American Numismatic Association
P. O. Box 2366
Colorado Springs, Colorado 80901
Publication: *The Numismatic* (monthly)

American Numismatic Society
Broadway, between 155 and 156 Street
New York, New York 10032
Publication: *Numismatic Literature* (semi-annual)

Paperweight Collector's Association
47 Windsor Road
Scarsdale, New York 10583

Chinese Snuff Bottles Society of America (bottles made in China)
2601 North Charles Street
Baltimore, Maryland 21218
Publication: *Chinese Snuff Bottle Newsletter* (quarterly)

American Carnival Glass Association
1555 Blossom Park Avenue
Lakewood, Ohio 44107
Publication: *American Carnival Glass News* (5 times a year)

American Custard Glass Collectors
4129 Virginia Avenue
Kansas City, Missouri 64110
Publication: *The Custard Partyline* (3 or 4 times a year)

American Pencil Collectors Association
Sterling, Kansas 67579
Publication: *The Pencil Collector* (monthly)

Pewter Collectors Club of America
P. O. Box 239
Saugerties, New York 12477

American First Day Cover Society
P. O. Box 23
Elberson, New Jersey 07740
Publication: *First Days* (bi-monthly)

Antique Collector's Club of America
Questers Antiques
210 S. Quince Street
Philadelphia, Pennsylvania 19107
Publication: *The Questers* (quarterly)

Wedgwood International Seminar (Ceramics)
c/o Mr. Byron A. Born
55 Vandam Street
New York, N.Y. 10003
(National organization for local society of collectors, specializing in 18th century ceramics.)

Christmas Seal and Charity Stamp Society
c/o Miss Jocile Maret
1906 Murphy Avenue
Joplin, Missouri 64801
Publication: *Seal News* (monthly)
Check Collector's Round Table
P. O. Box 27112
Cincinnati, Ohio 45227
Publication: *The Checklist* (quarterly)
World Wide Avon Bottle Collector's Club
P. O. Box 8683
Detroit, Michigan 48224
National Button Society of America
Box 116
Lamoni, Iowa 50140
Publication: *National Button Bulletin* (bi-monthly)
Beer Can Collectors of America
P. O. Box 9104
St. Louis, Missouri 63117
Publication: *BCCA News Report* (bi-monthly)
American Bell Association (Bell collectors)
Route 1, Box 286
Natrona Heights, Pennsylvania 15065
Publication: *Bell Towers* (monthly)
American Bottle Collectors Association
P. O. Box 467
Sacramento, California 95802
Publication: *The Pontil* (monthly)

INDEX